THERE IS NO BAD BEHAVIO[...]
"LEARN TO LIVE WITH."
EVERY DOG CAN BE WELL TRAINED
AND CAN BECOME YOUR LOYAL, LOVING BEST FRIEND.

FIND OUT . . .

- WHY PUNISHMENT CAUSES MORE PROBLEMS THAN IT CURES . . . AND THE CARING SYSTEM OF CORRECTION THAT REALLY WORKS
- WHY YOU MUST NEVER ALLOW YOUR DOG TO SHOW AGGRESSION TOWARD YOU OR ANY MEMBER OF YOUR FAMILY
- WHY IT IS GENERALLY A MISTAKE TO USE FOOD TO TRAIN A DOG
- WHY YOUR DOG REALLY DOES NEED A GOOD HUG EVERY DAY
- WHY OBEDIENCE TRAINING NOT ONLY MAKES YOUR LIFE EASIER . . . IT WILL MAKE YOUR DOG HAPPIER
- WHY A DOG DOES THINGS OUT OF SPITE—AND HOW TO CORRECT IT
- WHY ROUTINES AND CONSISTENCY ARE IMPORTANT TRAINING AIDS
- WHICH KINDS OF STRESS CAN HARM YOUR DOG'S HEALTH
- HOW TO DO "STUPID PET TRICKS" EVERYONE WILL LOVE

AND MORE!

101 TRAINING TIPS FOR YOUR DOG

101 TRAINING TIPS FOR YOUR DOG

KATE DELANO CONDAX

A DELL TRADE PAPERBACK

A DELL TRADE PAPERBACK

Published by
Dell Publishing
a division of
Bantam Doubleday Dell Publishing Group, Inc.
1540 Broadway
New York, New York 10036

Photographs by Susan Kuehnl and Mark Garvin

Library of Congress Cataloging in Publication Data

Condax, Kate Delano.
    101 training tips for your dog/Kate Delano Condax.
      p.   cm.
    Includes bibliographical references and index.
    ISBN 0-440-50568-2
    1. Dogs—Training. 2. Dogs—Behavior. I. Title. II. Title: One
hundred one training tips for your dog.   III. Title: One hundred and
one training tips for your dog.
SF431.C63   1994
636.7′0887—dc20   94-6387
                                                               CIP

Printed in the United States of America

Published simultaneously in Canada

November 1994

10   9   8   7   6

RRH

FOR

Blackie, Ursa Minor, Muffin, Ruffian, Big Red, Little Red, Feather, and Mildred

WITH SPECIAL THANKS TO

Laddie, Ralph, Winston, Buster, Boris, Graham Cracker, Annie, PeeWee, Bandit, Magnolia, Sport, Augusto, Eddie, and Rocky.

IN MEMORY OF

McSnoyd, Beauregard, Foxy, Sir, Skippy, Jeep, Hasso, Toby, Rose, Sadie, and Petunia

My sincere thanks to:

Robert M. Schwartzman, VMD, PhD, MPH
University of Pennsylvania Veterinary Hospital

Vicki Hearne
Writer and Dog Trainer

Dr. David T. Heller, VMD
Maple Shade Animal Hospital

Dr. Gloria B. Weintrub, VMD
AAHA Affiliate—IVAS Certified

Elizabeth Hugo
Hug-O-Bulls Bulldogs
Holly-Creek Kennels

Ken Hine, President and CEO
Kathryn Cochran, Manager of Association Relations
American Hotel & Motel Association

Susan P. Urstadt
Susan P. Urstadt Writers and Artists Agency Inc.

Jeanne Cavelos
Senior Editor, Dell Publishing

Cornelia Guest

Susan Kuehnl

Mark Garvin

Beth Skobel

Allan and Randi Waldman

Nancy Lovell

Karen Forrest

Frank and Gerri Shepard

American Automobile Association (AAA)

British Airways

Delta Airlines

Cunard Lines

Kim Krohn
Endangered Breeds Association

The National Dog Registry

Judith and James Yeargin

Sarah Crayton

Rick Guenther

Lt. Col. Arnold Francis Andrew Decker, USA (Ret.)

LDC and JB

CONTENTS

HOW TO USE THIS BOOK

You want your dog to do certain things (come when called, for instance) and not do other things (such as chew up the furniture).

Your dog wants to do certain things (such as sharpen his teeth on the handy tables and chairs in your living room) and not do other things (such as be interrupted and ordered to come to you just when the chewing is getting particularly interesting).

There is only one way to bridge the communications gap between humans and dogs. This method is *training*. Training gives both you and your dog a language in which to communicate with one another. Without it, your dog thinks your commands are arbitrary and confusing, while to you the dog's behavior seems disobedient or incomprehensible. Training makes life happier at both ends of the leash.

The introduction of this book is divided into two parts. The first part, "Principles of Dog Behavior," tells you how a dog thinks and what motivates him. Read it first; it will make training your dog much easier for you. The second part, called "Principles of Training," gives you a framework for all work you will do with your dog.

After reading both sections of the introduction, you will be able to turn directly to the problem(s) you want to correct, which are arranged alphabetically in the main section of the book. I hope this book will help make your relationship with your dog a happier and healthier one.

INTRODUCTION

This introduction will acquaint you with the basics of dog training and behavior. If you already know these, you can skip ahead to the main text. But if you're not sure, this information will help you succeed with the techniques explained later in the book.

PRINCIPLES OF DOG BEHAVIOR: WHAT MOTIVATES A DOG?

PACK INSTINCT

What does your dog want most in life?

Above all, he (or she) wants to be safe. He wants to know that the group he lives in, which includes himself, you, other members of your human family, and any other pets you have, is not in danger of being harmed or destroyed by any other group or individual.

Your dog is the direct descendant of millions of wild dogs who all felt this same way. Nothing you do will eradicate this strong feeling, the instinct for survival as part of a group.

Over millions of years, dogs who were members of packs with weak or stupid leaders did not survive to breed. Those who were members of well-led packs often did survive to breed, however, passing on the instinct to the generations that followed, including your dog. You must understand and work with this instinct.

In an orderly pack, the leader is the smartest and often, but not always, the strongest dog. Under him or her is a dog who can boss every dog except the top dog, and so on down through the pack. At the very bottom of the pack is a dog who cannot boss anyone and has to obey every other dog in the pack. Each dog obeys the dog(s) above him and bosses around those below him on the scale.

Each dog must find his or her place within the pack. This is done by testing the other pack members. Testing can take many forms: A dog can bite or snarl at another dog and try to make him run away or lie down in a belly-up position, which says "I give up. I admit you are the boss over me. I believe this so much that I will turn my belly up toward you so you could bite it if you wanted to, because I will do whatever you say from now on."

Or a dog may simply indicate by subtle body language that he believes himself to be superior over the dog he is challenging. He may, for instance, simply stiffen his legs and move "like a table, walking" in slow motion toward or around another dog that he wants to intimidate. If the other dog flattens his ears down against his head and lies down exposing his belly, the first dog has won. If the dog being threatened thinks *he* is higher in rank, he will grab for the neck of the challenging dog and a dog fight will ensue. Whoever wins the fight will be the winner. From then on, the higher dog will be able to intimidate the lower dog merely by walking up to him and assuming a challenging posture (such as the stiff-legged walk) or even just by looking sternly at him.

These power games may seem rather pointless when you live not in the wilds surrounded by wolves, lions, or bears but in a house in a town. Yet *all* dogs, regardless of how tame they are, are motivated by pack instinct. They all want safety in their lives. And the only way they can feel safe is if they know they have a strong, smart leader to their pack. *This leader must be you.*

Your dog will challenge you to see whether you are smart enough or strong enough to be a safe choice for pack leader. Different dogs will challenge you in different ways. A big, strong, rambunctious dog may try to prevent you from doing something he doesn't like (such as putting your hand near his food bowl when he is eating) by growling at you or even biting. A tiny dog can behave in exactly the same way. A dog with a less bold temperament may simply roll over and expose his or her belly when you come near, "asking" you to please be the pack leader and boss him or her around. Your dog could challenge your right to be pack leader by refusing to do what you say, whether it is expressed by not coming when called or not heeling when you are on a walk.

Dogs see things as black or white, yes or no. If your dog does not obey you completely, he does not accept you completely as pack leader. This means that in an emergency he will use his own judgment rather than do what you tell him to. In "civilization" this could have very bad consequences. A dog who decides to use his own judgment instead of following yours may decide to bite the intruder who is breaking into your home—perfectly sound thinking for a dog, but not good thinking for a "pack" living in a town where the meter reader has to get into the house and will sue you if your dog bites him. Because of the way we "civilized" people have set up our way of living, it is safer for a human, not a dog, to make the choices. *Therefore, you must be top dog at all times and under all circumstances, and your dog must accept your position without question.*

HOW DO YOU GET TO BE TOP DOG?

You get to be top dog by acting very like a dog does, challenging your dog and making sure you win. Your method of challenging him is a bit different, though. Whereas two dogs challenge each other by stiff-legged standoffs or fighting, you use a series of very effective situations that are set up so you will be sure to win. Yes, it *is* stacking the deck against your dog. It is making sure, in advance, that you will win, because you cannot accept anything less than your dog's complete acceptance that you are boss dog. You must win each challenge. Each challenge you make to your dog leads to the next one. Your job is to progress through the entire series of challenges and win every one. The process is called obedience training. It teaches your dog that in every situation he must do what you say, even though he might not have done things that way if left to his own choices.

What happens when a dog fully accepts you as top dog? A huge burden is removed from his mind: He has tested you in all sorts of situations, and in each one you have made sure that he did what you said, whether he agreed with you or not. He knows that you are stronger and smarter than he is, because you insisted he do as you said, even when he resisted. He now knows that you are trustworthy to head the pack and will make good decisions, and he can relax and simply do what you tell him or what you allow. He doesn't have to be constantly vigilant for danger outside the pack; you, as leader, will do that. All he has to do is do your bidding. It is reassuring to him and a big load off his mind.

AFTER SAFETY, FOOD IS OF GREATEST IMPORTANCE TO A DOG

Food is one of the most important elements in a dog's life. If you consider a dog's average day, you can see why: His life consists mainly of food, walks, training, and pats or hugs, with a lot of sleeping in between these activities. Of all these factors, food is the only one that your dog absolutely cannot do without;

in its extreme state, lack of food would end your dog's life. So, instinctively, your dog knows food is of life-or-death importance.

One of the first lessons your dog needs to accept and learn thoroughly is that he must never question your judgment even if his food is involved. This means you must be able to take up his food bowl at any time, even when he is eating. You must be able to reach into his mouth when he is chewing and remove a delicious morsel from between his very jaws (necessary when he accidentally gets hold of something that can harm him, such as a sharp bone). He must show no aggression *ever* toward you or any other person in your family. You establish this acceptance on the dog's part by training, using lessons that teach this. (See "Aggression.")

It is generally a mistake to use food to train a dog. Because the dog is very much interested in food, the practice works, up to a point. But in teaching basic obedience work (come, sit, stay, down, heel), a dog trained with encouragement and pats and body hugs will pay better attention to the work itself and not be thinking the whole time of how to con you out of a food handout. A dog trained *without* the use of food will begin to take real pleasure in the work itself and, like an athlete or dancer, will do it right because he enjoys doing something well. In this ability to concentrate on perfection—say, learning to come with unbounded joy when called—a dog outshines a human being almost every time.

THE IMPORTANCE OF A DOG'S NOSE

The inside of a dog's nose is like a crumpled-up sheet of thin paper. It is so convoluted that if it were flattened out, this area would be larger in surface than the entire outside surface of the dog.

Dogs use their noses far more than their other senses—sight, hearing, or touch, for instance. A person, on the contrary, uses sight almost exclusively to gather information. It is important to remember this difference when working with your dog. Your natural tendency will be to expect the dog to respond as you do, by *seeing* something and reacting to it, whereas the dog will almost invariably *smell* it and react to it.

A dog sniffing around a tree or lamppost smells not only which other dog was there, but how long ago, what sort of frame of mind that dog was in (happy and relaxed, anxious, angry and aggressive) and "reads" this information and remembers it. His nose "reads" the area for further information: How big was the dog, which direction did he go in from there, was he traveling alone or with a person or another dog?

You may find all his careful sniffing of the ground boring—after all, you are only able to gather information by means of seeing it. The best you, a human, can hope to *see* is that the ground is damp and thereby deduce that a dog may have left his mark. But you won't know the "fine points" your dog reads with his nose.

For this reason, it is important to allow your dog enough time to sniff his surroundings sufficiently. If you insist that he always follow you in "heel" position, you deprive him of his main system of taking in new information about his surroundings. Preventing your dog from sniffing is, to him, the same as making you walk around your neighborhood blindfolded. Give your dog plenty of time to walk using the full length of a four-foot lead.

PRINCIPLES OF TRAINING: A FRAMEWORK FOR ALL YOUR WORK WITH YOUR DOG

CORRECTIONS FOR MISBEHAVIOR: HOW MUCH IS ENOUGH? SHOULD YOU PUNISH YOUR DOG?

There is a big difference between *punishing* your dog and *correcting a mistake he has made.*

Punishing a dog makes him feel bad and think that he is a bad dog. It makes him become ashamed and sad. It may make him become so discouraged that he will become tricky and try to find ways to get around your general disapproval. Punishment spreads a deep gloom. It is not useful in training.

Correction for misbehavior is very different. A correction is specific for a specific problem. It lasts only long enough to change the behavior, then it disappears as if it never existed. The dog feels that he is a basically good dog who has made a mistake, that you do not like the mistake but you still like him. Therefore he is more likely to try to change the behavior, both to please you and to make his life more pleasant.

Here is an example to illustrate the difference between punishment and correction.

Let us say that your dog is reasonably well house trained. Yet one day, for no apparent reason, he leaves a puddle on the middle of your living room floor. You are quite upset with this. Why, you wonder, is your dog suddenly going backward in his training? Why is he doing something he very well knows is wrong? After having the dog checked by a vet to be sure the problem is not caused by a medical problem you decide to make sure he gets the message loud and clear that this will not be tolerated.

A person who *punishes* this dog will do something like this: He spanks him, yells "No!" at him, sticks his nose in the spot, takes him outside, and continues to scowl and say unfriendly things to the dog. Then he brings the dog back in, perhaps more angry than ever because the dog refused to make a proper puddle outside where he was supposed to, puts the dog into a kitchen or bathroom—confining him to "teach him a lesson"— and leaves him there to ponder his mistakes.

However, a person who *corrects wrong behavior* does this: He spanks the dog, yells "No!" at him, sticks his nose in the spot, and takes him outside. But here is where the difference lies: Now he changes completely from strong disapproval to *total approval,* as if nothing had ever gone wrong. He says "Good dog!" and pats him, chats amiably to him, goes to some interesting trees or bushes, makes a show of sniffing around them as if scenting who's been there before. When his dog does even a little puddle, this person praises him enough so he knows he has done right, but not so much that the dog gets embarrassed. If the dog, still upset from being corrected in the house at the scene of his crime, does not make a puddle outside, the owner takes him inside, gives him a pat, and ignores him. If the dog comes over, asking for a pat, he pats him.

The owner can then return to the spot on the living room rug alone, without the dog (who may watch from a safe distance in another room, or may hide in another room, fearing more correction) and pretend to be sniffing it, saying *"Not nice!"* in a loud voice. Then the person will go back to what he was doing (reading, watching television, working) as if there had never been a problem.

The dog learns, from the second description, because it *corrects the bad behavior* but does not punish him or make him feel that he is inherently bad. (Being inherently bad is being unlovable. If you won't like him no matter what he does, why should he even try to please you?)

However, the dog does *not* learn from the first description, which punishes the whole dog in a general way. Punishment

simply makes a dog feel inadequate and asha...
not show him what he ought to do to please y...
show a dog what you *do* want him to do every tin...
what you *don't* want him to do.

WHAT IS "ENOUGH" CORRECTION?

Enough correction is *just enough to get the result you want,* no more. You should use as gentle a correction as you can. For instance, with a shy, humble dog you might simply say in a very disgusted tone, "Oh, what a disgusting thing to do. *Not nice!*" This dog would be corrected sufficiently not to do the behavior again. But with a more confident dog, or a downright stubborn one, you might find that the mild correction won't work. After you had tried it once, the dog would wet the living room floor again. So you would increase the amount of correction, giving him a sturdy whack on the thigh with your hand, sticking his nose in the wet spot, saying "Bad dog!" loudly. But in both cases, no matter how strongly you correct the dog, *you cease the correction the moment you have made your point.* That is, when you take the dog outside after correcting him, you act as if nothing had happened. You praise the dog. (This tells him that wet spots inside on the rug are not okay, but wetting the grass outside is encouraged.)

Use this same system of correction in all your work with your dog. Use just enough correction to get the job done, no more. Cease giving the correction as soon as you are sure you have made your thoughts on the matter clear to the dog. Always ask yourself: "Could I use *less* correction with this dog than I ught? Could I stop giving the correction *sooner* than I thought?" *The least amount of correction for the shortest possible time is what you want.*

HUGS AND PATS

Good solid body hugs (putting your arms around your dog's chest or neck and torso) give your dog a feeling of security and appreciation. Just as people feel proud at work or school when they do something well and are singled out for praise, or when they receive an unexpected compliment, hugs satisfy a need in dogs. Dogs like to feel proud of themselves, just as everyone else does. You bond your dog more firmly into your "pack" (headed by you as pack leader) by giving him hugs from time to time.

You can give a dog a hug and verbal praise when he does something especially well (such as catching a Frisbee and bringing it back on command, or jumping through your arms when made into a hoop). Do so any time when you want to say to your dog, "You're a great dog, and I'm glad to have you in my pack." Words do serve somewhat the same purpose, but a body hug goes further and reaches some part of the dog that words do not.

The only dog you must *not* hug is one who is so traumatized or frightened that he may bite. For this situation, training is necessary to remove the causes of fear or aggression. Then these dogs, too, will be good candidates for a hug. (See "Aggression" and "Biting Human Beings: Fear-biting.")

Good solid body hugs are reassuring to your dog.
They make him feel loved and appreciated.

THE IMPORTANCE OF ROUTINE

If you do things the same way over and over, a dog learns what to expect and is reassured by this. Your dog will be happier and more relaxed if he knows that he will be fed at about the same time every day than if he expects dinner at a time he is used to, doesn't get it when he expects it, worries that maybe there won't be any dinner, and finally is fed, but only after he has felt hunger pangs and worried for a few hours.

Changing the schedule once in a while won't do irreparable harm. Suppose you are late coming home one day. It won't kill your dog to be fed a bit later, especially if you reassure him with words and pats that you didn't mean to upset him.

But in general, try to adhere to a schedule that is fairly consistent. This is especially important if you are rehabilitating a frightened or insecure dog (such as some dogs adopted from animal shelters, or dogs who have been abused), as routine makes all dogs feel more secure. Routine shows insecure dogs that there is a pattern to their life with you rather than a jumble of events and frightening happenings.

Routine begins the process of showing the dog that the world you create for him is governed by logic. Therefore there is a way for the dog to function in this world that makes sense to him. *Routine is the beginning of establishing a language between you and your dog.* It lays the groundwork for the next stage, which is training. (Training creates a highly useful language between people and dogs.)

WHEN THINGS GO WRONG IN TRAINING

When you are teaching your dog new work, and you come to a point where either you cannot get the dog to see what you want, or he stops doing the new work even though he had begun to do it previously, always do this: *Go back to the last thing the dog learned before, and repeat that.* Then praise the dog. Then try the new work again.

If you succeed in getting the right response in the new work, praise him again. If the dog seems confused or reluctant, go back to the previous work, accomplish that, praise him, and let it go for another day.

For example, let's say you are teaching your dog to jump through your arms when held like a hoop. (See illustration, p. 198.) Suddenly he won't even try. He hangs his head and sits down, despite encouragement from you. You go back to the previous achievement: You set up a little barricade only a few inches high, have the dog jump over that, and praise him. Always quit on a happy, positive note; make sure the last thing your dog does before you quit training is something he does well, and praise him for it.

EQUIPMENT YOU SHOULD HAVE FOR TRAINING

You will need these pieces of equipment to train your dog effectively:

- *Chain choker collar,* just big enough to slip easily over the dog's head. The smaller the links, the better, as it makes the chain slide more easily. (See "Collars.")
- A *jumping bat,* used for riding horses. Similar to a riding crop, but much more sturdy. Often made of rubber covering over fiberglass center, with a tab of rubber. (See illustration, p. 140.) Sold in tack shops for about $10 to $15.
- A *four-foot leash,* strong enough so it cannot break even under extreme conditions. Sold in pet stores.
- A *fifteen-foot leash,* called a longe line, with sturdy safety snap (like those found on leashes). You can make this yourself from rope and a snap. Be sure the snap is large and strong. Attach snap to one end, and tie a hand-loop at the other. Sash cord, sold in hardware stores, is stronger than clothesline rope. Snaps also sold in hardware or marine (boating) stores.

Types of Leashes
Top: Rolled Leather Leash
Middle: Cloth Webbing Leash
Bottom: Longe Line (extra-long) leash

101
TRAINING
TIPS FOR
YOUR DOG

ACUPUNCTURE

Acupuncture for dogs can be helpful in relieving conditions such as hip dysplasia, arthritis, muscle spasm, nervous disorders, vertebral disc disease, chronic skin allergies, respiratory disorders, vomiting, diarrhea, cardiac problems, and acute injury to ligaments. It can help boost the immune system.

Once considered a "quack" cure without medical benefit, today acupuncture is recognized for the valuable and useful procedure it is. Before you commit your dog to surgery or drugs, you may want to try it. I know of a number of cases where acupuncture was performed on dogs that had been given up as lost causes, with spectacularly good results.

Acupuncture is fully approved by the American Veterinary Medical Association (AVMA). The procedure can be used in combination with conventional medicine. Doctors of Veterinary Medicine (VMDs) state that acupuncture "can help treat practically any disease" but stress that a veterinarian must first evaluate the dog before treatment.

A list of VMDs who are qualified practitioners of acupuncture can be obtained by calling or writing to: International Veterinary Acupuncture Society, 2140 Conestoga Road, Chester Springs, PA 19425. (215) 827-7245. The list contains the names, addresses, and telephone numbers for 350 certified acupuncturists worldwide. For certification, veterinarians must pass a 120-hour course, an oral and written examination, and casework. Their certification must be renewed periodically.

Acupuncture is among the oldest systems of healing in continuous practice in recorded history. The procedure, which involves insertion of extremely fine needles into the body, stimulates specific points that have the ability to alter biochemical and/or physiological conditions, allowing the body to heal itself. In Western medicine, acupuncture is most often used to relieve pain and is resorted to after conventional medicine has failed. But on three-quarters of the world's population, acupuncture may be the *first* treatment used. In China, for instance, which has one-quarter of the world's population, acupuncture has been in use for six thousand years or longer.

Acupuncture works primarily through the central nervous system, increasing circulation, causing release of neurotransmitters and neurohormones, relieving muscle spasms, stimulating nerves, and stimulating the body's defense mechanism, among other effects.

It is not painful because the extremely fine, solid needles are designed to enter the skin with almost no resistance. Most dogs actually relax as soon as the needles are in place. One dog I know of used to jump happily onto the acupuncturist's table and lie down and sigh contentedly, knowing that his pain was about to disappear.

Variations of technique in acupuncture include *electroacupuncture* (stimulation by gentle electrical impulse), *aquapuncture* (injection of a solution at key points of the body), and *acupressure* (pressure on the skin at key points).

The success of acupuncture varies with the disease or condition being treated. Large joints, for instance, generally respond more successfully than small joints. As with all medicines and procedures, a small percentage of the population fails to respond at all; this is approximately 5 percent with canines. In some cases, the condition initially will seem to grow worse, but such cases often reverse themselves dramatically. In each case, proper evaluation by a veterinarian before treatment is an absolute requirement.

ADOPTING A DOG

If you adopt a dog from a shelter, find a dog as a stray and adopt him, or even adopt a dog from someone you know, the dog may be upset or traumatized, depending on what bad experiences he has had. Add to this, problems in getting used to a new set of circumstances, learning a new routine, and becoming acquainted with new people and location, and it will be clear why many dogs show problems of adjustment when adopted.

Fortunately, even a badly upset dog will, with proper patient care, learn to trust you. Some badly frightened dogs eventually become absolutely wonderful friends and companions, but it takes time (a year or more in some cases).

The rewards of rescuing a hurt, lost, abandoned, or traumatized dog are great. But it *is* work to overcome the obstacles.

The most important thing to do with an adopted dog is to make him feel safe and secure. Give him his own bed and his own place to eat. A *crate* is a good place for both sleeping and eating. (See "Crates.")

Be certain the dog cannot get loose. Traumatized dogs will seek opportunities to dash out an open door and will not come when called, due to fear. For this reason, keep a collar and leash on the dog at all times, even in the house, except when in his crate.

When you leave the dog alone, put him in his crate and make the door extra secure by securing it with a metal snap (like those found at the end of a dog's leash) at both the top and bottom of the door. Some dogs will push their way partway out of a crate even with the door latched shut unless you secure the door at the top and bottom.

Be sure that you remove the dog's choke collar and any other collar before you put him in the crate, as they can get caught and choke the dog. As an added precaution, be sure all doors are shut to the room in which the crate is located before you put your dog into or take him out of the crate.

Keep an identification tag on the dog at all times; the only exception is the time he is in the crate; when in the crate he must not wear any collar or other equipment of any kind. (See "Identification Tags and Tattooing.") As soon as you bring him out of the crate, put his collar with identification back on at once.

Keep the dog's environment as free of turmoil and stress as possible. Rowdy children, noisy television, shouting, rough play by another dog all upset an already stressed dog. A quiet, calm, well-ordered routine will help undo the stresses your dog has undergone before you got him.

Feed and walk the dog at roughly the same times every day. Routine is soothing to a dog's spirits.

Move slowly and speak quietly around a traumatized dog. If he will allow it, give him gentle body hugs, but do not hurry to do so if they seem to upset him. Remember, it takes time for a badly traumatized or upset dog to gain confidence.

When your dog is fairly confident in you after the first few days, take him to the vet for a checkup and any needed vaccinations or treatments. Put *two* collars and two separate leashes on him; a frightened dog can slip a collar and escape. Use one choke collar, just big enough to slip over the dog's head, and one webbing or leather collar with identification tags attached adjusted as snugly as possible so it cannot slip over the dog's ears if he suddenly pulls backward. He may well do this in the upsetting environment of a vet's office.

If your dog shows any tendency to fear-biting (see "Biting Human Beings: Fear-biting"), put a muzzle on him before you take him into the vet's office. The kind made of Velcro is easy to adjust (adjust it to the right size for his muzzle before you leave the house; but actually put the muzzle on the dog just before you get out of the car, so he won't have to ride in the car wearing it.)

Your dog takes his behavior cues from you. Be patient, clear in your directions to him, kind, and calm.

ADOPTING OUT A DOG
(FINDING A HOME FOR A DOG)

It is perfectly possible to find an excellent home for a dog you must give up or for a stray you rescue. The dog's life literally depends on you, and there are risks inherent in the process. These can be overcome by consistent work and diligence. The rewards are great; one of the nicest sights you will ever see is that of a dog you have placed with wonderful new owners, who, when you visit at a later date, hides behind his adoptive family so that you will not try to take him back with you.

Dogs, if they are healthy and docile, are worth money to various institutions including medical schools, dental schools, and pharmaceutical companies, which use them as expendable commodities and put them to death, and for certain illegal uses, such as bait for making dogs fight for gambling purposes, among other even more ugly examples. (See "Dognapping.") You need to be fully aware of this danger before you place a dog. By charging an adoption fee of at least $60, you minimize the risk of someone's responding to your notice with intent to sell the dog.

Three of the best places to advertise a dog for adoption are newspapers, veterinarians' offices, and pet supply stores.

Find a newspaper serving neighborhoods where you think your dog would be safest and most happy. Get the rates for a dog adoption advertisement (usually somewhat less than for other want ads). List the characteristics of the dog: *breed* (or type); *age* (approximate if you don't know); *sex* (and whether neutered/spayed/housebroken); *temperament,* especially with children and other pets. Add your area code and telephone number, and use the phrase "Try-out basis."

A typical ad might read:

> **Adopt ($60 fee) Golden Retriever**
> **mix, male, neutered, 4 years,**
> **housebroken, loves kids,**
> **not good with other male dogs.**
> **Very playful.**
> **(212) 555-7899. Try-out basis.**

For vets' offices or pet stores, make up a flyer, preferably with a photograph, and photocopy it in color.

Some of the telephone calls you get may be from real potential homes. Some may be from the simply curious ("Why do you want to give the dog up? I once had a dog like that . . ." etc.). Some may be from people with dishonest purposes in mind. These professional con artists call all adoption dog want ads every week and impersonate legitimate would-be owners. They are skillful. (It is their business to be convincing.) The men and women sound nice, they give you the "right" answers, and you may find yourself leaning toward giving away your dog for free. Be warned: By doing so you can very possibly be sentencing your dog to a painful and distressing death.

Here are essential checks to make prior to giving serious consideration to potential new owners:

1. Ask for the name and telephone number of their veterinarian. *Call the vet.* If he or she is busy, ask a time when your questions can be answered for the purpose of placing a dog, and call back. Find out how long the would-be owners have been clients of the vet, how reliable the vet judges them to be, what happened to their last pet (if the vet tells you it was run over by a car, beware), whether they got routine vaccinations and heartworm preventive medicine, and anything else the vet can tell you. Ask if the vet thinks every member of the family would welcome a dog. (For instance, the vet may know that the wife loves dogs but the husband hates them, or that the children are prone to let dogs out by accident.)

2. Require two pieces of identification from the prospective owners. Be sure one has a photograph if possible. Ask for a utility bill giving the owner's address. See if it matches what the people say.

3. Get a copy of the lease, if the people rent, to verify that the lease allows dogs.

4. Speak with all prospective members of the household, not only the one who answers your ad. (Do this before you actually take the dog to the house of the adoptive family.)

5. Have the dog neutered or spayed before you adopt him or her out. If this is absolutely impossible, get a deposit of $50 to $75 from the prospective owner, which you will refund when the dog is altered.

6. *Always visit the home in person prior to placing an animal there.* Look for potential dangers: doors that open onto the street without a second doorway to prevent the dog from running out are one of the greatest dangers. Other potential hazards include windows on high floors unprotected by guards; dangerous household items in places where a dog could get at them (see "Household Items That Can Harm

Your Dog"); cold, damp, or dark basements where the new owner intends to keep the dog; holes in a fence around the yard the dog will be turned out in; or places he can dig under a fence. (See "Pens and Fenced Enclosures.")

There is one rule I always use in adopting out a dog: If you have any doubts about the people, do not give them the dog, even though you had thought they were good candidates before. Tell them that you cannot give them the dog now, that you will contact them after the dog has a final treatment at the vet's, or anything else necessary. But if you have a "bad feeling" about people, even if you cannot put your finger immediately on the reason why, you should listen to your hunch.

When you find truly wonderful owners, you will have none of these qualms about giving them your dog. Everything they say and do will indicate strongly and convincingly that they are responsible, careful, caring people who will give the dog a safe, comfortable, and loving home.

Here is a sample list of questions you should ask anyone who responds by telephone to your advertisement for a dog. As you ask the questions, you want to give the people plenty of chances to talk without letting them know, by your tone of voice or the way you phrase your questions, what answers you hope they will give. For instance, if you ask in a sympathetic tone of voice "How do you exercise your dog?" a person may say "We let them run loose" whereas if you ask "You don't let your dogs run loose, do you?" a person may well say "Oh no, never," because they know that that is what you want to hear.

1. *Have you ever had a dog before?*
   Beware of people who say they have had dozens of dogs. This can mean that they let them get killed on highways, had gotten rid of them when they became inconvenient

or when they moved or had children, or other irresponsible reasons.

2. *What happened to that dog?*

   Many people with dishonest purposes in mind know that the "right" answer to this question is that the dog died of old age, indicating that they took good care of him for his entire life. So don't place too much value in the answer. But ask it anyhow; you sometimes learn something about the people.

3. *How do you usually give your dog exercise?*

   As above, people who want to sell dogs after adopting them know that the "right" answer is "We walk him on a leash. We do not let dogs off the leash. We do not leave dogs unattended even in our fenced yard. We never tie a dog up even for a moment when we go into a store."

4. *Does your husband/wife/housemate like dogs?*

   Beware of people who say "No, not especially, but I will be the one looking after the dog." A spouse who hates dogs can accidentally let them out.

5. *Is anyone in your family allergic to pet hair?*

   Many children are.

6. *Who is your veterinarian? Do you mind if I call him/her for a reference?*

   Beware of anyone who objects to this. A legitimate person will welcome the good reference they know the vet will give. If someone objects, rule him or her out immediately.

7. *Do you have children? What ages?*

   Determine if the ages and temperament of children and dog will be a successful match. A skittish or frightened dog, such as one you rescued, may not get along well in a family with young, active children; at worst, the dog could run away or be teased until he snapped at a child. Don't try to force-fit a match; find a true match between family and dog that is as stress-free as possible.

8. *Will you mind showing me two pieces of identification, one with a photograph?*

   Rule out people who balk at this; they may have given you a false name. (See box, p. 11.)

9. *What kind of work do you do? What does your husband/ wife do?*

   If one spouse is often on the road and the other works outside the home full time, who will look after the dog? If no one will be home for longer than eight or ten hours at a time, rule out situations like this.

10. *What will you do with the dog when you go on vacation?*

    People who say they will take the dog along *may* be a risk —the dog could get loose and lost in a strange place. Using dog-sitters or boarding kennels is a better choice.

11. *Do you mind if I visit the dog periodically after you adopt him?*

    You will need to make at least one follow-up visit to see how the dog is being cared for; rule out anyone who says he objects to this question.

If you get no responses to your advertisement or flyers, or none that you like, try the ad again in another place. Some community newspapers run an ad for seven days in several different newspapers owned by the same company for the cost of one insertion. Ask around and find the names of newspapers in your area (the local library is a good source), then call their classified advertising department for rates.

You can find a home for a needy dog if you are persistent enough and keep doing the steps just outlined until it *does* work. In twenty years I've never failed to find a home for a stray, although sometimes a dog has been returned as many as, in one case, six times before he found the perfect home; another was returned to me after a year and a half when the new owner broke his back in an accident.

When you find a perfect-sounding candidate on the phone, have gone to investigate his/her home and found it checks out

NOTE: VERY IMPORTANT!

Write to the United States Department of Agriculture (USDA) to get a list of federally licensed animal dealers in your state. The address is: USDA Docket Reprints, VS REAC, Room 266 FB, 6505 Belcrest Road, Hyattsville, MD 20712. Animal dealers routinely sell animals to research facilities, medical schools, dental schools, and pharmaceutical companies. While the list isn't a foolproof method of identifying all animal dealers—new ones aren't added immediately—it can sometimes give you information to screen out con artists who intend to adopt your dog only to sell it into a particularly cruel death.

Check the names of people responding to your dog-adoption advertisement or flyer against the list. *Be sure you always check any name of a potential adopter by looking at two pieces of identification, one showing the person's photograph, the other showing his or her address.*

in a positive way, met all members of the family and felt they would be a good match for the dog, observed the dog for an hour or so in their home and seen that he seems reasonably content there, and have made the decision to give a trial adoption to the people, you need to do one final thing.

You must make sure the adopter signs a written adoption agreement. (A sample follows.)

ADOPTION AGREEMENT

_____
(Date)

I, _____ , residing at _____ agree to adopt
    (name of adopter)   (street address, town, and state)

from _____ the dog described below:
    (your name)

_____.
(dog's sex, color/and markings, age, spayed/neutered, breed or mix if known, weight, hair type: long/short)

I agree to return the dog to _____ in event that I can no longer keep him/her. I
        (your name)

promise to notify _____ if this happens and to bring the dog to _____
        (your name)   (your

_____ . I will not under any circumstances give away or sell the dog to another person,
name)
animal shelter, organization, or institution.

If I intend to move from the above address, I agree to notify _____ of my new
        (your name)

address and telephone number.

I agree to be fully responsible for the safety and well-being of this dog. I will be repsonsible for
routine veterinary care, emergency medical care if necessary, food, and all other care for the
well-being of the dog. If at any time injury, loss, or death of this dog occurs, I am obligated to

notify _____ immediately.
    (your name)

I agree to spay/neuter the dog within three weeks of adoption. I agree to pay an adoption fee of
$60.00 (sixty dollars) prior to taking possession of the dog.

I agree to hold blameless _____ from any and all claims of liability for the conduct
        (your name)
of this dog upon my possession of him/her. This applies to all known, unknown, and unforsee-
able damages resulting from my adoption and ownership and control of this dog.

This is a binding contract, enforceable by civil law.

Signed,

_____
(Adopter's signature)

_____
(Adopter's name, printed or typed)

_____
(Address of adopter)

_____
(City, State, Zip code of adopter)

_____
(Home telephone of adopter)

_____
(Your signature)

_____
(Your name, printed or typed)

AIR-CONDITIONING AND YOUR DOG

In the heat of summer, especially in cities, where the average temperature can be as much as ten degrees hotter on a given day than in surrounding areas, air-conditioning is a good solution to having a happy, physically comfortable dog.

If you work during the day, leave an air conditioner turned on at the lowest setting. A dog, even one with thick fur, such as an Akita or husky, will be comfortable while at rest (and your dog sleeps most of the time when you are not around and nothing exciting is going on) in temperatures as high as 80 degrees.

Do *not* leave a window open instead, unless it is securely fastened to open no more than a few inches. Like a small child, a curious dog can wriggle through it and escape or fall to his death. If you do open a window for ventilation, put a nail or fastener, available in hardware stores, to make sure it cannot open more than four inches (even less for a Chihuahua!).

Make sure that the vents from the air conditioner are pointed away from the dog's bed. Point the air flow slightly up from the level of the air conditioner, and turn the other vents to the side (away from the dog). This is especially important if your dog stays in a crate while you are out. A dog subjected to any draft (from a fan or air conditioner) can become sick or even die.

Before you leave the dog alone, test the temperature of the room after twenty-four hours of running the air conditioner at the lowest setting, to be sure that it produces the temperature you expect. Also check the air conditioner's plug; if it is hot to the touch, have an electrician replace it with a three-prong plug. A plug that becomes hot to the touch can cause a fire and is dangerous, not only to your dog but to your entire home.

Bear in mind that dogs with very short hair, such as pit bulls or Chihuahuas, will feel the cold a lot more than their furrier brothers and sisters.

Blocking direct sunlight will help keep your rooms cooler and cut down on the amount of air-conditioning you need. You also can cut costs by utilizing the "economy" setting found on many air conditioners, which causes the machines to shut off automatically when the proper temperature is reached.

For dogs who are active outside (who jog with their owners or play with other dogs in a fenced-in park area, for instance), it is more healthful if the temperature they live in inside the house is not drastically different from the outside temperature. Thus dogs will be healthier if, in a city where summer temperatures regularly reach 90 or 95 degrees, the temperature in the house is kept at 80 or 85 degrees, rather than at 70.

It is a kindness to your dog to maintain reasonable temperatures for him when you are at home and when you are not but he is there, if at all possible. Air-conditioning makes this possible.

AGGRESSION

AGGRESSION WITH CATS

If aggression with cats occurs outside, while you are walking your dog, use the same correction as for "Aggression with Other Dogs."

If you own cats, however, and want your dog to learn to live with them, the correction is different.

Attach your dog to something inside the house that he cannot possibly move no matter how hard he pulls, such as a radiator or a doorknob of a strong door. Don't use the leg of a table or bed, as a strong dog can move these if determined.

Let your dog see the cats from a distance. If they eventually walk by, in sight of the dog but out of reach, your dog will probably begin straining to get near them. If he does this, take the flat of your hand and slap him flat on the top of his head with your palm. Make the slap sharp and hard enough so he momentarily stops paying attention to the cat and pays attention to you. If he continues without pausing to try to get at the cats, you haven't slapped him nearly hard enough.

As you slap him on the top of the head, say sharply "Hey!" When he stops momentarily, say "Good dog" but keep your voice soothing rather than enthusiastic; the dog is already over-excited, and you want to calm him.

Be ready for him to make a second lunge at the cats (if they have not disappeared by now), and repeat the correction every time he shows aggression toward them or even toward the area where they are hiding. If he strains his leash and pulls in the direction the cats have gone, correct him.

Look at your dog's ears. If they are up, he is thinking about going after the cats, and he should be corrected. Only when your dog flattens his ears against his head has he given up the idea of attacking the cats. Now he is saying to you "Okay, I agree not to chase the cats because you have said not to, and you are the top dog in my pack."

Having two crates side by side, with the dog in one and the cats in the other, may help the dog to get used to them. (See "Crates.")

Do not trust your dog alone with the cats until every sign of aggression is gone. While this may take weeks or even months, most dogs can be trained successfully to leave cats alone. In time many even become very fond of one another.

AGGRESSION WITH OTHER DOGS

A dog is aggressive for a reason: He is defending himself, possessive of his toys or bowl, territorial of his turf, trying to get rid of competitors for a mate, afraid (as in the case of small dogs in the presence of a much larger dog), or, in rare cases, in pain.

Whatever the cause, you *must not* allow your dog to be aggressive with other dogs or with people. (See also "Aggression with People.") If you do allow your dog to show aggression with other dogs, he will quickly assume that you have given up your role as pack leader and that it is all right for him to make up his own mind on this and other matters. Signs that your dog is showing aggression toward another dog may include one or more of the following: walking stiffly, standing stiffly (sometimes with tail held high and wagging stiffly, sometimes with tail held still), furious barking or growling (except in cases that are clearly a game and in fun), snarling, standing motionless over another dog in an intimidating way (perhaps growling at the same time), or an outright attack or lunging at another dog.

Note: By lowering his front end while his back end remains standing up (see illustration, p. 18), your dog is assuming the "Let's play!" position. Even though he may also bark, this is *not* a show of aggression. This play position is universal in dogs.

If a dog is known to be aggressive with other dogs, it's wise to have a choker collar and leash on him in advance. The moment he shows aggressive behavior, bellow "Hey!" or whatever word you choose to mean "Stop doing what you are doing this instant!" You can use "No!" or "Out!" if you prefer, but be consistent. You must always use the *same* word to mean "Stop that right now!" I have found that dogs easily understand "Hey!" because it is sharp and can be said with real force more easily than other words. Be sure to yell loudly; it will shock your dog, tends to intimidate him, and gets his attention.

As you say "Hey!" pull upward on the leash, which will

"Let's Play!" *Position.*
This is universal canine body language.
*It is **not** aggression.*

tighten your dog's choker collar. With a small dog, one hand will be enough to pull upward on the leash. With a large dog, use both hands. Pull upward until the dog's *front legs* are off the ground at least five or six inches in a small dog or a foot or so in a large one. Hold him in this position for about eight or ten seconds while you repeat "Hey!" about once each second. This reinforces the command; it teaches the dog that "Hey!" means stop the behavior or something you don't like will happen to you. Then let him down; he should gag or even try to throw up. This is normal. Watch to see if he shows submissive behavior (ears flatten down, he looks away when you say "Hey!" again). If he shows any aggressive behavior, repeat the whole process at once.

Is this cruel to the dog? Absolutely not. It will not harm him at all,* but it will be extremely unpleasant for him. Because of the fact that in the excitement of showing aggression, your dog will pay less attention to you than in most other training situations, you must make your point clearly—that you do not allow aggression, no matter how justified the dog may feel in showing it, and that you will correct it swiftly and surely if he goes against your wishes.

What *is* cruel to any dog is being inconsistent in your correction, thereby confusing him. This will happen if you fail to do your job—swift, decisive action every time your dog shows aggression toward other dogs. Inconsistency in training makes dogs confused, frightened, and angry because there is no way they can know what is and what is not allowed. Inconsistency is the number-one cause of neurotic, badly behaved dogs. Be absolutely consistent.

As stated by William Koehler, the great American dog trainer: *The dog is entitled to the consequences of his own actions.* If you follow the rules for correcting aggression with dogs, your dog will learn quickly that although he may *feel* like showing aggression, the penalty is too severe, and he then will *decide for*

---

* Do not use this correction on a dog who is sick or very old, however.

himself not to show aggression. In effect, he says to himself: "I really hate that other dog, and I'd like to bite him into little pieces, but my pack leader says for me to stop saying horrible things to him and be quiet. I'd better do what the pack leader says or he will make things more unpleasant for me than I am willing to put up with. It's just not worth it to show my aggression when I hear the word 'Hey!' "

Note: If the other dog is on a leash, tell the other owner to pull his dog away from yours. If the dog is loose, pick up a small rock and throw it at the loose dog, and yell "Git!" at him, or threaten him with a stick if one is handy. Often this will be enough to discourage a loose dog from picking a fight with yours or from responding to your dog's aggression.

Another correction for aggression is as follows: Make the aggressive dog sit facing you if possible. Grab his cheeks, one in each hand, and lift him up from the sitting position while shaking his head from side to side. Look straight into his eyes (this intimidates a dog) and *holler* at him *"Bad dog!* Hey! Don't you do that to me!" The words don't matter as much as the sincerity with which you tell him, *as loudly as possible,* that you really don't like his behavior. But do *not* attempt this correction if your dog shows signs of aggression with people.

For less serious crimes, you can do this: Make the dog sit, facing you. Pull up on the leash, attached to his choker collar, until his head is as high as it can reasonably go without pulling his front feet off the ground. Using your hand, palm upward, come from about the dog's chest level sharply upward with your hand and hit the dog sharply under the chin. You can't harm him this way, but it is very unpleasant to the dog. At the same time, stare menacingly at him, and use the command words as just described.

When you have corrected the dog, reinforce your message—that you are top dog and that he must obey you—by facing him sideways, reaching under his body, and, with one hand grasping the front and the other hand grasping the back legs on the *far* side of his body, pulling them abruptly toward you. (See illustration, p. 22.) Do it with a sudden jerk, and the dog will topple over on his side. Then pin the dog, upside down, to the ground, by grasping his skin on either side of his neck, pinning him down with one knee, or whatever is required to keep him in this position. Hold him there for several minutes, no matter how much he tries to get up; with a very resistant dog, hold him down for a full half hour. Almost any dog will "give up" and concede victory to you within that time.

While keeping the dog upside down, do not talk to him and certainly do not pat him. From time to time you could draw your teeth back in a snarl and growl at him menacingly. This reinforces your "top dog" status, as this correction is almost an exact duplicate of the way dogs and wolves reinforce their hierarchy in the wild.

See also: "Fights Between Dogs."

AGGRESSION WITH PEOPLE

Fortunately this problem is not difficult to cure. The earlier you take action to correct a dog's attempts at aggression with people, the more easily you will change the dog's mind about it. If you hesitate or are wishy-washy about making the correction, you will be allowing the dog to continue the wrong behavior, and the job of correcting will become more difficult. Act swiftly and decisively at the *first* sign of aggression. (See also "Biting Human Beings.")

If your dog growls at you (unless he is clearly playing, in which case he will probably lower his front end onto his elbows, while his back end remains standing in the universal dog body-language signal for "let's play!"—see illustration, p. 18), stiffens his body in a threatening way when you approach his food bowl, or raises his lips in a snarl, he is showing aggression. If you fail

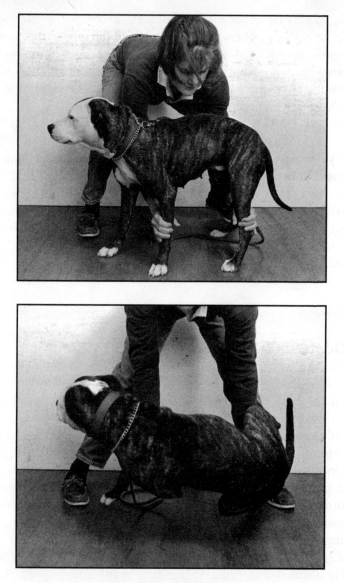

Toppling a Dog Over
This will make even a stubborn dog lie down.
It also establishes your dominance over the dog.

to correct the early signs of aggression, the behavior may quickly move to the next step, biting.

What you do to correct the behavior depends on circumstances. If the dog is on a leash, pull upward on it as in the correction given for "Aggression with Other Dogs." If there is no leash on the dog and water is available, fill a glass with hot tap water and throw it forcefully in the dog's face. (Be sure the water isn't so hot enough to scald him; you should be able to put your own hand into it and hold it there for three seconds.) As you throw the water, aim for his mouth. At the same time, say "Hey!" loudly.

If there is no water available and the dog is not on a leash, take a large book, perhaps 12 inches by 10 inches, and a quarter-inch or less thick, and hit the dog squarely on top of the head with the flat surface. (A children's book works well.) If it is a big, strong dog, use a fair amount of force; if it is a small dog, use less.

What is the "right" amount of force? Just enough to make the dog stop showing signs of aggressive behavior.

Do not praise the dog after a show of aggression has ceased. Instead, make him obey a command such as "Sit!" and *then* praise him by saying "Good dog!" once. The reason is, the dog must know that nonaggression toward people is the normal, all-the-time way to behave. He doesn't get praise for doing what he should do all the time. But he does get corrected for doing what he must not do—showing aggression. He gets praised only for performing a command such as "Sit!" when told to do it.

If you feel you cannot deal with your dog's aggression, hire a good dog trainer at once. Do not delay, hoping the problem somehow will go away by itself; it won't. It will escalate into biting unless you take immediate action. You should give yourself a chance to try the correction first, however. Often you'll achieve the desired result much quicker than you might realize.

Note: If your dog shows aggression only when you try to approach his food bowl when he is eating, do the following: When you feed him, do not put the bowl down on the floor. Instead, hold it in one hand and, with the other hand held flat, feed him his food handful by handful. When he will eat without showing aggression, put the bowl closer to the floor, keeping one hand, palm upward, in the bowl while he eats. If he growls then, throw a glass of hot water into his face, say "Hey!" pick up the bowl, and feed him handful by handful again. Do this for a few days or even weeks, until he shows no signs of aggression.

Caution: Never try to put your hand near a growling dog or one who is "frozen" and looking at you with a threatening look. If you have any doubts about a dog's intentions or attitude toward you, hire a professional dog trainer.

Be sure that you recognize aggression and do not mistake a dog who nips you with love or a dog who "talks" by making friendly growling noises for one who is showing aggression. An aggressive dog's behavior seems to say "I am angry, and I am going to tell *you* what to do. I do not intend to respect you as my pack leader." One test you can try is to yell "Hey!" at a dog you suspect of aggression. If he flattens his ears and acts in a submissive fashion, he is not showing aggression. If he simply pauses for a moment, then continues the behavior *without* flattening his ears or showing submission, he probably is showing true aggression. If you're not absolutely sure, call in a professional trainer.

There is another, unorthodox cure for aggressive behavior in dogs that works extremely well with some dogs and may be worth a try. Some toy stores and novelty shops sell "fun trick noisemakers," or *poppers* or *bomber snaps.* These are very small amounts of exploding powder wrapped in tissue paper, about the size of a lemon seed, but rounder. When thrown on the floor, they make a sharp snapping sound. If you try this remedy with an aggressive dog, be sure to throw the bomber snap onto the floor at least two feet from the dog so there is no chance it will touch him. Do this as soon as he shows the first sign of aggression. As you throw it down, yell "Hey!" so the dog will learn that he'd better pay attention to you when he hears the word.

Some people recommend filling a soda can with pennies and shaking it or throwing it on the floor near the dog. In my experience, this does not work very well, but it may be worth a try, particularly with a dog who is shy by nature.

Another remedy some people find useful is spraying Bitter Apple (sold in pet stores) at the dog's nose (while saying "Hey!" at the same time). This may help with some dogs.

Note: With puppies under a year old, begin at once to roll them over onto their backs and hold them there for a few seconds, by their legs and with a hand on the puppy's stomach. This teaches that you are the boss, the pack leader, and that when the puppy submits to your domination, nothing bad happens to him. Do this from time to time a few times a day until he accepts the action without protest. With larger dogs, you can reinforce your position as pack leader (a dog who accepts you as pack leader will not show aggression toward you) by doing the following, called the *long stay.*

Place the dog in down position. (See "Down!") Get down on the floor beside him and crouch over him, facing in more or less the same direction. Grasp one of his forearms in each hand and hold him down by hovering over him. (See illustration, p. 26.) If he tries to get up, hang onto his arms and lean down over him with the weight of your body. Keep him in this position, without talking to him except for command words ("Down!") as needed. If he is likely to chew on your hands, wear heavy gloves and do not attempt to correct him right now for chewing on you. Keep to the main correction, which is to immobilize the dog for a *full half hour* on the floor, against his wishes. This proves to him that you are the boss and that you must be obeyed. Doing so can have far-reaching, positive effects on your dog's behavior in general.

Note: Do *not* try this correction if you think the dog may attempt to bite your face. In such a case, use the correction given in "Aggression with Other Dogs."

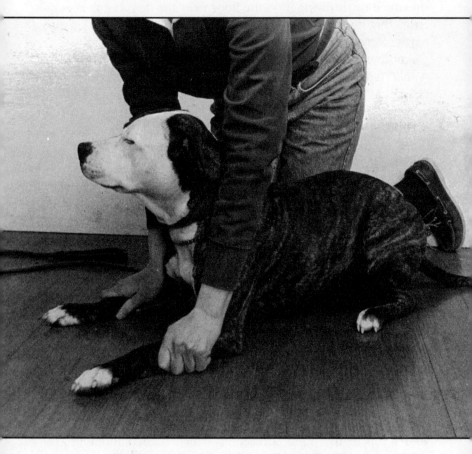

Holding a Dog in a Long Down Position
This establishes dominance over the dog.

AGGRESSIVE DOGS:
HOW TO FRIGHTEN THEM AWAY
WHILE WALKING YOUR DOG

One of the most annoying things to happen on a walk with your dog is to be threatened or attacked by aggressive dogs who are left loose by irresponsible owners. If you see a loose dog who is acting aggressive (barking, growling, stalking you in a stiff-legged walk, or running at you), act without delay.

Pick up some rocks, big enough to fit into the palm of your hand—the bigger the better—and throw them toward the attacking dog. Try to make the rock bounce on the ground in front of the dog, rather than aiming for a direct hit and missing the dog altogether. If you are unlikely to find loose rocks where you walk, always carry a few in your pocket, just in case. Throw several in rapid succession.

A good-size stick will also deter a menacing dog. Hold it in the air and brandish it as if you mean to beat the daylights out of the dog. If you carry a pooper-scooper, this may serve the same function.

As you use either rocks or stick, yell horribly in your most frightening and loudest voice. Shout "Go home!" Usually such tactics will scare off a bothersome dog. If your dog enthusiastically joins you in trying to frighten off the aggressor, give him a sharp tap on the head with your hand or lift his front end off the ground for a few seconds. (See "Aggression with Other Dogs.") You do *not* want your own dog to attempt to "help" you put the other dog in his place. He must leave this to you.

If a fight ensues despite your best efforts, see "Fights Between Dogs."

Most aggressive dogs who are loose (when your dog is properly on his leash) are nothing more than bothersome, posturing frauds. Usually they will not actually attack, especially if you act aggressively yourself (with rocks, stick, and voice).

Never try to run away from aggressive dogs. Doing so will encourage them to attack. If you stand your ground and make more fuss than he is making, an aggressive dog will nearly always leave you alone.

ANAL RUBBING

If your dog sits down and drags himself forward, scraping his anus against the ground, his anal sacs may have become impacted.

Anal sacs are located on each side of the dog's anus. If they become clogged, the normal secretion, a thick, dark, and smelly liquid, cannot escape.

Use disposable rubber gloves for this job. Hold the dog's tail straight up with one hand. With the other hand, cover the anal area with two or three layers of tissues. Then place a forefinger and thumb on either side of the anus, slightly lower than center. (Imagine the face of a clock; place your thumb where the eight would be, your forefinger where the four would be.)

Squeeze gently until liquid spurts or drips out from each gland. Be gentle; your dog's whole tail end is already irritated by the impaction.

If there is any sign of blood or pus, see your veterinarian, who will complete the job and prescribe antibiotics, as infected anal sacs can cause systemic infection.

See also "Worms."

APARTMENT LIVING WITH YOUR DOG

What can you do to adapt an apartment so it is safe and convenient for living with a dog? (Much of the following also applies to house-living as well.)

First, remember that a dog is like a two-year-old child. Like a small, active, and curious child, a dog will explore and demolish, chew on and play with everything in your apartment. And like a child's understanding, a dog's understanding of certain important things is minimal or nonexistent.

WINDOWS

Be sure windows are shut or that a dog cannot open them in an attempt to wriggle out. A dog has no understanding of the height of your windows above the ground; there is nothing in a dog's evolution that prepares him for the possibility of living so far from ground level. While waiting at the veterinarian's, I once witnessed *three* separate cases, two dogs and one cat, of animals who had fallen from high windows. The question is not why the animals were stupid enough to go out an open window, but rather why the owners were too ignorant to keep the windows shut as they would for a small child.

Most dogs will push through a screen; this is not a safe barrier between your dog and a fall.

FLOORS

Neighbors below will be glad if you use wall-to-wall carpeting or an abundance of rugs to cover bare floors. A dog's nails clicking on the neighbor's ceiling is a major annoyance to many people.

POISONS

Because space is limited in an apartment, and because many apartments need pesticides or bug traps from time to time, you may have these in your apartment. Be sure to store them on a very high shelf where your dog cannot possibly get at them, as a dog may open a cupboard or closet while you are out and empty it. Bug traps can taste good and be fatal to your dog.

TRASH

Most dogs love to root through trash or garbage if you leave it where they can get at it. Since you may put bones in garbage, and in any case will be less than pleased to come home to find a mound of trash spread all around the kitchen, it makes sense to keep trash and garbage in the only place out of reach to the dog but readily accessible: on top of the refrigerator.

CRATES

Crates for confining a dog while you are out of the house or apartment are a good idea, especially in apartments. (See "Crates.") Be sure to put your dog's crate in a place where sun will not beat down on it while you are out, as being trapped in hot sun with no means of escape could make your dog uncomfortable or even frantic.

BAD BREATH

Bad breath in a dog seems like almost a joke; you are tempted to ask the dog "Oh, boy, what have *you* been eating?"

But bad breath in dogs is not a laughing matter, because a genuine problem underlies it. Your aim must be to remove the cause, not to attempt to cover up the bad odor with mints, sprays, or other surface treatments.

Bad breath is probably caused by one of two things. Either the teeth are beginning to decay, or the dog has a systemic condition (such as an infection in the throat or stomach). Dogs who eat feces can also burp disgustingly with a foul odor, but this, unlike the other two examples, will usually occur only when he has just eaten feces. The other two cases are chronic.

The first thing to do when your dog exhibits bad breath is to have him thoroughly checked by a veterinarian. If his teeth are decaying, or he has an abcess, a vet will clean the teeth, pull the tooth if necessary, and make sure that there are no hidden areas where decay can continue to cause trouble.

If cleaning the dog's teeth does not eliminate the bad smell, the vet will check further for systemic problems.

If you have any doubts about your vet's ability to determine the cause of the problem, go to a large animal hospital, such as the one at the University of Pennsylvania in Philadelphia or the Animal Medical Center in New York City. Only recently have many vets recognized veterinary dentistry as a crucial aspect of canine health, and not all vets are as good dentists for dogs as others. You might ask for a veterinarian board-certified in the practice of canine dentistry. This means he or she has passed strict examinations in this specialty. (There are also board-certified vets for other aspects of canine health.)

Once the cause of your dog's bad breath has been removed, you can keep his teeth clean yourself. Bend a nail, or simply use a sharp knife. Get your dog used to having his teeth cleaned by making the first several times very easy for him to tolerate. That is, don't actually scrape his teeth very much, and keep him still for only ten or twelve seconds.

To do the procedure, make your dog lie down. (See "Down!") Then make him lie on his side. He will be more likely to cooperate if you ask him to lie down on something soft and comfortable, such as his bed or a rug.

When he is on his side, make him place his head flat on the floor by gently but firmly pushing down on his face. (Be sure not to press on his eye.) Praise him as you do this.

Then, while holding his face down, gently lift his lip away from his teeth with the other hand. Start scraping with the canine teeth ("fangs"), then move back to the molars. You will have to stretch the skin a little to expose the molars.

At first, just get the dog used to having your hands on and around his teeth. After about ten seconds, let him get up (say briskly "Okay!" so he knows the session is over). Then in a half hour or so, repeat the process. This time scrape very gently on the canine tooth for one or two seconds.

Each time you repeat the procedure, do slightly more. Finally you will be able to clean any tooth by scraping it until the brown tartar, which forms near the gums, is removed and the teeth remain white and shiny.

Remember that you must take care not to jab the dog's tender gums accidentally. To do so will quickly destroy his confidence, and you will have to begin training again at the beginning.

With patience you should be able to achieve your aims, however. Even frightened or aggressive dogs have learned to cooperate in this procedure.

If you find that you absolutely cannot accomplish it yourself, take your dog to a board-certified dental veterinarian every year, and have the vet clean his teeth for you.

BARKING

All dogs bark sometimes—a bark at the right time can save a dog's life or that of you or your child, or your property. There are numerous well-documented accounts of dogs having saved the life of a family member.

But dogs who wile away the lonely hours by barking simply to amuse themselves can be a real distress to neighbors. Therefore, it makes sense to teach your dog not to bark aimlessly when you are out of the house or apartment. The two ways to do this both work well.

The first involves more time, but costs nothing. Dress for work or to go out in the normal way. Pick up your keys as usual, walk out the door, lock it, walk away, and wait. Stay as far from your front door as you can, being sure you can still hear your dog if he barks.

The moment you hear *any* noise, either a bark or even a small whine, rush back to your door, open it, say "Hey!" loudly, and either throw a glass of water at your dog or swat his thigh with your jumping bat. (See illustration, p. 140.) If he is in a crate, bang on top of the crate with a book or jumping bat to make as much noise as possible for three or four seconds.

If the dog hides in another room, do not be tempted to fail to correct him, saying to yourself "He obviously knows he has done wrong, so why punish him further?" Unless you correct him, he will not make the decision in his own mind that he *must* not bark when you are out. He will know that you don't like his barking but will still think that it is "worth it" to bark if he feels like it.

Your job is to make the option to bark when left alone *unacceptable* to your dog. He must say to himself: "I'd like to bark for a while, but if I do, I will have a swat with the jumping bat on my rear end. It just isn't worth it. I'd better be quiet instead."

As soon as you have given the correction with the water or bat, go out immediately. Do not pat or praise the dog, or try to comfort him. Just leave, as before, and repeat the exercise.

When you can wait for five or ten minutes without any sounds coming from your dog, return home, but do not make a fuss over your dog. Just say "Good dog!" once or twice, and go about some other business for a while. This tells the dog that your coming and going is nothing special, and he will be encouraged to accept it in a matter-of-fact way.

You also can leave a tape recorder running (get the longest-running tape you can find) when you leave. Play the tape back later to see if your dog has been absolutely quiet. Try this when you go to work the first few days after beginning this training.

A second method of correction requires that you buy a fairly expensive piece of equipment, an *antibark collar,* and adjust it correctly. Your veterinarian can tell you where to buy one. Most are sold by mail order, and they cost somewhere around $100. A battery fitted into the collar gives the dog's neck a small but unpleasant shock when he barks. (The vibrations of the bark activate it.) These can be useful to correct a dog who barks only after he hears your car drive away. The collars come in different sizes for large and small dogs.

The drawbacks, besides cost, are that the collar is heavy and, if used continually, can cause hair loss around the neck. The good news is that these collars sometimes work exceptionally well. Often after a few days or weeks of use, they can be removed for most or all the time. Dogs are smart; they soon realize that even if you have removed the collar, you could put it back on again, and therefore they choose not to bark.

A third possible option is one I strongly advise against. Some people have their dog's vocal cords removed. When the dogs bark, only a hoarse huffing noise comes out. I'm against this operation because the anesthesia is dangerous, your pet can have complications from surgery, it removes his natural voice forever (think how you'd feel yourself—I believe dogs are very upset by this loss) and it is really awful to see a dog in this condition. There is also the chance that sometime, somewhere, your dog could be in a life-threatening situation where only his bark could save him, or you.

Note: To train a dog who will not bark at all (some very shy dogs will not) to bark when strangers come to the door, do the following.

Have a friend come to your door and ring your doorbell or pound loudly on it with his knuckles. Begin barking yourself, in an excited way. Show agitation toward the noise, and pay a lot of attention to what you are doing. Pay no attention to your dog, but show him by example what you consider appropriate behavior when someone comes to your door.

If your dog does nothing, just ignore him, and let your friend repeat the exercise. Bark enthusiastically, as before.

If your dog lets out even a little whimper or a tiny bark, praise him and give him a body hug, and keep barking. Gradually even a shy dog will learn what is expected and that you approve of his barking.

Be very sure, however, before you train a dog to bark that

you really do want him to do so. It isn't fair to change your mind, once he has learned to bark, and decide he has to be quiet after all.

BATHS

Grooming parlors for dogs can make your life easier. You simply turn over your dirty dog to them and you get back a clean, sweet-smelling pooch. But the cost can be considerable, and there is a practically no-cost alternative: Give your dog a bath yourself. It is a lot easier than you may realize.

Put your dog into your own bathtub, fill it with warm—not hot—water, wet the dog using a spray attachment or a small saucepan to ladle on water, rinse thoroughly, and rub dry with a towel.

Use either baby shampoo or special-formula canine shampoos from your veterinarian. If your dog has fleas, use a flea shampoo, also available from your vet.

If your dog is likely to jump out of the tub, attach him by a short leash to the tub's faucet handles; be sure you allow him only a few inches of leash, or he may manage to jump out anyway.

If he is at all likely to try to bite you, put a muzzle on him before you begin. But also follow instructions for "Biting Human Beings," and train him not to bite under any circumstances.

When you finish his bath, he will want to shake off vigorously even after you dry him as much as you can with towels. Make sure he is not near any prized porcelain or glass possessions, as many dogs will "scoot" around at top speed, delighted with their clean fur, for a few minutes after a bath. If the weather permits it, you may want to take your dog for a bike ride immediately after his bath. This both dries him and allows him to burn off excess energy. (See "Bicycle Riding with Your Dog.")

BEDS FOR DOGS

Your dog needs a warm, soft, comfortable bed of his own, away from cross-traffic of people and other pets going back and forth, and out of drafts.

Pet stores make round beds for dogs that resemble giant pillows. The soft fiberfill pillow is covered by a removable zippered cover that can be washed. Also available are similar shape beds filled with cedar shavings, which mold to a dog's body and smell good.

If your dog has any tendency to chew (almost every dog does this until at least two years of age, and some continue much longer), you can fold several old towels in half. These can be washed readily, and if chewed they can be refolded to prevent bare spots.

A good place for your dog to sleep at night is in a crate (see "Crates"), but you must remove any and all collars before he goes into it. You will need another bed for daytime use, where your dog can lie down for naps at will. On cold, hard floors, such as cement floors, place cardboard or plywood beneath the bed to prevent chill from seeping through.

CIRCLING BEFORE LYING DOWN

Most dogs will, before they lie down, circle two or three times. Periodically a sleeping dog will wake drowsily, get up, and circle again before going back to sleep. This is not an attempt to get the snakes out of the grass. It is merely a way for the dog to get circulation going on the side on which he has been lying. It also helps the dog to arrange his new position with his head facing north. Most dogs will position themselves facing north when they sleep; studies have shown circulation improves, heartbeat slows, and metabolism improves when the body is aligned with the earth's magnetic field.

BICYCLE RIDING WITH YOUR DOG

If you can ride a bicycle with confidence, you may want to try riding with your dog. This provides one of the most enjoyable methods of exercise for dogs, and it yields another benefit to the person riding the bike: admiration. Dogs admire feats of strength and endurance because packs that were led by strong leaders survived the rigors of the wild and passed this characteristic on to modern-day dogs.

If you ride your bike with your dog, the dog will consider you "cool." He will be amazed by the endurance that lets you not only go as fast as he can, but even faster, and farther. This makes a big impression on a dog.

Get a sturdy bike. Attach a leash on the *left* side of the bike, on the post that holds the seat up. Do not attach the leash anywhere else or you risk certain disaster. Attaching it to the

Bicycle Riding with Your Dog
Attach the leash to the post underneath the bicycle seat by making a loop through the leash handle.

Keep the leash from turning around the post by passing it through the bike frame. Then wind the leash around the post until it is short enough . . .

*. . . so the leash cannot reach farther forward
than the hub of the bike's front wheel.*

handlebars, for instance, is a recipe for suicide. So is trying to hold the leash in one hand.

Be sure that the dog's head, when facing forward and pulling slightly on the leash, can reach no farther than the center of the front wheel. If he can reach any farther forward, he may turn the front wheel and cause you to fall. If you cannot find a way to shorten the leash (which is easily accomplished by tying a loop in it), make a leash by tying a snap onto a length of clothesline rope. (Use two such leashes if your dog is strong and big.)

Most bikes have springs under the seat. Slide the leash through these and make sure it comes out from the back of the bike, not the front. Unless you do this, the leash will rub against your left leg when you ride.

When you want to go forward, simply move off, and the dog will follow. You may want to say an encouraging word to a timid dog and give him a pat.

Always ride facing traffic (on the "wrong" side of the street). This keeps your dog as far as possible from cars. It gives you a chance to pull off to the edge of street or sidewalk if a car approaches too fast or fails to allow you enough room for safety.

To turn right, just turn as usual, and the dog will follow. To turn left, however, you need to warn the dog that you plan to turn the bike in his direction. Say "Git!" sharply, put your left foot at his shoulder, and push him gently as you turn. The dog will quickly learn the meaning of the word and turn for it alone.

To stop, simply apply your brakes.

If you attach the leash as described, the balance is so secure that even a large dog lurching after a squirrel cannot pull you over. The only time you are vulnerable to being pulled over is when you have stopped.

Keep a stick and some small rocks in your basket or pocket to discourage loose dogs (nearly all towns seem to have some) who may attempt to chase after you. Generally a rock thrown in the direction of a loose aggressive dog is sufficient to send him away. Yell "Hey!" at the offending dog at the same time, and

Turning Left

Put your left foot gently against the dog's shoulder and push him to the left, away from the bike. Say "Git!" so he learns the verbal command at the same time.

appear as aggressive and threatening as you can. If your dog attempts to chase a squirrel, say "Hey!" and tap him sharply with your toe, enough to get his full attention.

Caution: Start off by going slowly (at a dog-trot speed) and only for a block or two. Gradually build up the speed and length of ride as your dog becomes more fit. Too much too soon could give your dog sore feet, sore muscles, or strain his heart. Be sure you do *not* bike with your dog on very hot days, especially when it is humid or, in cities, when the air is polluted. Let your dog guide you in determining when "enough is enough." Don't overdo it; slow down if you even *think* he may be tired. Some dogs learn to signal you that they want to slow down by nuzzling your leg; some will slow down and pull back slightly; but some will slow down only after you have slowed the bike first. Therefore, slow the bike frequently to test whether your dog is ready for a slow trot.

I have bicycled with a dog for over thirty-five years without a mishap. Once you know how to do it, it works just as well with three, four, or even five dogs at the same time. Dogs like it so much, because it gives them physical exercise while letting them see something interesting and smell all the interesting smells around town, that they quickly learn to cooperate with you. It makes all your other training work easier, because your dog will be physically and mentally relaxed, and because he will have something he enjoys enormously to look forward to.

"Escape artist" dogs—those who regularly slip out open doors and roam the neighborhood—will almost always change their agendas dramatically when taken for bike rides. Many dogs are simply bored by being kept in one location. Try being cooped up yourself for a few days; you too will long for the wide open spaces and slip out a door yourself! Dogs love bike-ride runs because they tend to be longer than on-foot walks, and they give the dogs a chance to see something entirely new and smell some entirely new smells on foreign turf. Many confirmed escape artists become model citizens when bike-ride-walks become part of their schedule, and are actually glad to be home

You can bike with one dog . . .

*. . . or two, three, or even more dogs,
once they learn what is expected.*

again to have a good rest after covering a couple of miles at a trot.

Note: When biking with your dog, be sure to stop from time to time near a tree, telephone pole, or pile of leaves so your dog can leave his mark. See "Marking."

In summer, bike early in the day before the sun gets hot, or after the sun sets. Wet your dog's head before you go to help him remain cool. Dogs are prone to heatstroke if overheated. Use common sense.

BITING HUMAN BEINGS

Biting people is perhaps the most serious of dog crimes. It almost always happens because someone failed to correct a dog when he first showed signs of aggression toward people. All normal dogs can be trained to respect human beings and learn that they must never, under any circumstances, bite them. Even a dog who has actually bitten a person can be retrained successfully.

The only exception is the *extremely rare case* of a dog with a brain tumor, thyroid malfunction, or other physical cause, which can contribute to erratic behavior. If you have any doubts, get the advice of a professional trainer and/or a veterinarian.

For a dog who bites or attempts to bite people, follow correction for "Aggression with Other Dogs" and "Aggression with People."

Note: Little nips with the front teeth only are *not* aggression. They are a sign of the highest degree of affection or love. Your dog is saying "You're so wonderful you're good enough to eat!"

If the nips hurt, discourage them with a tap on the top of the dog's head with the flat of your hand, just hard enough to cause him to cease the behavior. Then give him a body hug and praise him, so he knows you don't like the way he is showing affection, but you still like *him*.

FEAR-BITING

Fear-biting is just what it sounds like: a dog biting because of extreme fear that amounts to panic. Dogs who have been cruelly abused, beaten, terrorized by human beings, or tortured can show signs of fear-biting. Some dogs are born timid, and naturally fear everything in life. Luckily, even dogs who are fear-biters can be retrained with patience and kindness.

If a dog cowers down and shows his teeth in a snarl when you approach, particularly if he is cornered or in a crate, he may be showing signs that could lead to fear-biting. A fear-biter must *not* be punished; he is already so distraught that punishment will make the problem much worse. Instead, he must be persuaded gently that you are a rational being who will act toward him along logical lines and will not harm him or cause him pain. The best treatment for a fear-biting dog is to sit quietly nearby, not making advances toward him but showing that you are friendly by speaking kindly to him from time to time. Another action that often reassures dogs is to "wag your tail"—that is, move your fingers against your leg similar to a dog wagging his tail. Many dogs "read" this signal as a friendly gesture; confident dogs will wag their tails in response. A timid or frightened dog may not show any overt signs of response at first, but the gesture will tend to reassure him.

When you feed a fear-biter, hold the dish of food in your lap rather than putting it down on the floor. Keep your hand, palm up, in the dish while the dog eats. Do not move your hand, just keep it there. Talk soothingly to the dog the whole time. Feed the dog small amounts several times a day so you multiply the number of feedings per day; the more the better.

It takes an abused dog a long time—months or even a year or more—to overcome bad prior experiences with human beings shocking enough to have made him resort to fear-biting. Fear-biting is not the dog's fault. It is entirely the fault of the person or people who so confused and frightened a dog that he felt he had no choice but to resort to extreme measures.

If you have patience and work consistently, usually you can retrain a fear-biting dog with very good results. However, if circumstances mimic the earlier bad experiences (for example, if the dog was beaten by children, he may never again trust children), remember that the dog will react initially with fear. At this point you must calmly remove the cause (ask the children not to come up to this dog, for example) and reassure the dog with voice and a hug that everything is all right.

If you are not comfortable doing the training yourself, a good professional dog trainer can help you. Contact one without delay. (See "Aggression with People.")

BLOAT:
SUDDEN UNEXPLAINED ACUTE INTESTINAL PAIN

Bloat is an avoidable ailment that will kill your dog if you do not get immediate medical attention. Bloat attacks without any warning when a previously healthy dog suddenly shows signs of acute distress.

Bloat most often affects big, broadly built dogs, although it can strike any dog. If you feed your dog a large meal (especially of dry food, followed by heavy drinking of water) and exercise him within an hour or two afterward, his stomach may twist over, cutting off the normal path of food through the intestine.

A dog with bloat will suddenly appear very restless, walking around, licking at his stomach, getting up and lying down repeatedly; he may drool or salivate and try to vomit. Nothing comes up after one or two tries, but a dog with bloat may continue to retch. His stomach, filled with food and gas, will be swollen.

Take a dog with such symptoms to a veterinarian or veterinary hospital *immediately.* Surgery is the only remedy for bloat. In some cases the stomach can be positioned correctly and attached to the body wall so it will be less prone to bloat in the future. Failure to take immediate steps to correct bloat will lead to shock and death.

A dog who has had bloat or shown any of these signs should be fed one of two ways: You can give him several small meals a day, with dry food already moistened thoroughly so the dog won't eat it and drink water afterward, which causes the food to swell. Or alternatively, you can give your dog free access to dry food at all times. Paradoxically, this reduces overeating because the dog realizes he can eat all he wants without fear it will disappear. However, if you are changing over from specific meals to the free-access method, watch carefully for a few days to be sure the dog doesn't overeat at first and get bloat from it. To minimize this risk, at first thoroughly wet the food you leave. Be sure to replace the moistened food frequently, especially in hot weather, so it does not spoil. When he is used to the system, replace the moistened food with dry food.

Always let your dog rest quietly after meals for at least two, preferably three hours. Rough play, strenuous runs, and turning him upside down on his back are all to be avoided after mealtimes.

Note: People who work during the day should exercise their dog first, when they return home, then feed him afterward.

BOARDING KENNELS

HOW TO FIND A GOOD KENNEL

When you have to go away without your dog for a few days or weeks, you will need to have a reliable boarding kennel to leave him in. (See also "Dog-sitters and Dog-walking Services.")

A word-of-mouth recommendation from people who have tried and liked a particular kennel is one of the best ways to find a good one. Also ask dog trainers.

Be sure to visit the kennel yourself before you leave your dog there. The place should look in good repair, be immaculately clean, and have no unpleasant odors, and the staff should be polite and businesslike.

Most kennels will not let you see the back part where the actual runs are, but some will. Ask if you can. Your dog should have an indoor-outdoor run. There should be a small room inside, preferably with a slightly raised wooden platform for sitting and sleeping on, connected by a doorway with a flexible plastic door to an outdoor run at least six or eight feet long and four feet wide. The floor throughout must be cement. (Otherwise dogs can dig out under the fence.) The chain-link fence must be heavy gauge and in good repair. A second fence outside the runs must be present as a second line of defense in case a dog actually escapes his run. A fencing cover over the top of the run, both inside and out, is desirable; most dogs do not climb chain-link fences, but some do. The presence of a fence-ceiling eliminates the chance of an escape artist's climbing out.

Some dishonest kennels keep a "visitors' area" where all is neat and clean, but do not maintain the actual living quarters of the dogs as well. Try to determine if this is the case when you visit the kennels.

In an emergency, you can board your dog at a vet's. Usually

this is not a good solution for more than a day or two, as most vets keep the dogs in crates and walk them only once or twice a day in a small pen nearby. Some employ young people to walk the dogs on the streets; this is risky. Also some vets keep boarding crates in the room with X-ray equipment, which can expose your dog to radiation.

A reputable boarding kennel will not object if you telephone often—even daily—to see how your dog is doing. A tip to the kennel workers at the end of your dog's stay will make them remember you in a positive way.

Before you take your dog to board, be sure he has his vaccination records for DHLPP and rabies, the two vaccination records required by all responsible boarding kennels. If you are *not* asked for these records prior to bringing your dog, do not use that kennel. Also have your vet provide a treatment against kennel cough before you leave your dog at a kennel. This preventive treatment is squirted into the dog's nose by the veterinarian. Kennel cough usually is not serious, but like a bad cold, it is unpleasant for your dog, and it can lower his resistance to disease. If your dog picks up kennel cough while boarding, he'll have to be treated. Prevention is the best medicine.

When you get your dog back, look for signs of ill-health such as chewed patches ("hot spots") on the skin; fleas; poor, thin condition; dull or fearful behavior. These are all strong warning signs; do not use this kennel again if these signs are present.

Take a soft bed or blanket or towels as a bed for your dog, and make sure the kennel attendant agrees to leave them in his run. Many kennels prefer not to leave things in the runs because they can get dirty and cause the workers extra work. You need to get a clear agreement on this in advance, or else your dog may end up sleeping on a hard wooden platform or even cold cement.

A sign that your dog has been well cared for at a kennel is if he is delighted to see you, alert and happy, and probably hoarse from barking (one of the chief entertainments at a boarding kennel); even dogs who are not allowed to bark indoors at home usually enjoy barking their heads off for a few days or weeks when away from home.

BONES: IMPACTION

If you feed your dog bones, buy only very thick beef shin bones, which cannot splinter and which are too hard for the dog to chew up completely. Avoid any but the thickest and heaviest shin bones, because a dog can crack and swallow thin or small bones. Avoid also the ends of the bones (the joint end) because dogs can chew these up and they may impact in their intestines.

Impaction can be life threatening. Your dog will show signs of extreme discomfort. He will not eat, will probably vomit, and may show signs of bloody diarrhea.

Take the dog to the vet immediately. In an extreme emergency where no vet is available, administer a half cupful of mineral oil through a special syringe. (You must get the syringe in advance from a veterinarian; it is much larger than ordinary syringes.)

See also "Bloat." Symptoms are similar.

Note: Rawhide chew-toys are usually produced in South American or Far Eastern countries, where regulation regarding the chemicals used in processing may differ markedly from U.S. regulations. Therefore I prefer to let my dogs chew on domestic cow hooves, which are harder for the dogs to chew up and less likely to contain toxic chemicals. Cow hooves make a good substitute for bones to chew on.

BONES: KEEPING GREASE OFF RUGS

If you give your dog bones as a treat, first read "Bones: Impaction."

Bones given in a house or apartment can ruin rugs, as dogs invariably choose a nice, comfortable place to lie down and go to work on it.

Confine your dog to an area where he cannot harm your rugs, such as the kitchen, but put down two or three old towels to make a cushion for him. If you stack the towels up, then fold them in half; the resulting square will be big enough for the dog to rest his elbows on it and will give him traction with the bone. When he is all finished, you can put the towels in the wash.

If grease does, nevertheless, get onto your rugs, first make a solution of a little dishwashing detergent in warm water. Scrub the patch, let it dry, and then scrub gently with Nature's Miracle. This odor remover chemically dismantles smells at their source. It's available at some pet stores and some veterinarians' offices. Don't use anything else. Most so-called odor removers leave odors of their own that are nearly as offensive as what they are supposed to remove. Nature's Miracle has next to no smell of its own, and it works wonderfully well.

BROKEN GLASS

If you see broken glass on a floor or on the ground on your walk, keep your dog well away from it. Small shards may lie unseen far from the major area of broken glass. A dog's pads are vulnerable to shards, which can puncture the sole of his foot and necessitate a trip to the vet.

If you find yourself practically on top of broken glass, however, simply walk through without pausing, but do *not* begin to pull your dog along and try to hurry him through it. If you pull, he may "put on the brakes" and resist, which will make it more likely that a piece of glass will be forced into his foot.

If your dog is small enough and you are sure he will not resist, pick him straight up and carry him over the area. Otherwise walk through instead.

If your dog begins limping and licks at the sole of his foot, suspect glass. Don't attempt to remove it yourself; it could break off in his foot. Take the dog to a vet.

CARS: CROSSING BETWEEN PARKED CARS

Parked cars represent danger to your dog. Even a car that appears to be empty could contain a driver who was merely bending down when you looked at the car and who suddenly starts the car and moves off. Especially in cities, where cars must be moved for street sweeping, and drivers are thinking about getting to work while they wait to move their parked cars to the proper side of the street, your dog is in danger if he is allowed to do his morning business between them.

Cars in parking lots that require the driver to back up in order to leave the parking space represent danger to you and your dog if you walk behind them.

Teach your dog to use the very edge of the sidewalk to urinate and defecate. (See "Curbing.")

When you must cross a street, cross at the corner; if you must cross in the middle of the street, check between parked cars, and check both of the cars you must pass between before stepping off the sidewalk with your dog.

This may seem excessive care for something so ordinary as crossing a street; but all it takes is one step between the wrong cars to end your dog's life.

CARS: ON THE STREET

Teach your dog to sit before you cross any street. This gives you time to look carefully before moving into the path of traffic. (See "Sit!")

When biking with your dog (see "Bicycle Riding with Your Dog"), always keep him on the left of the bicycle, and always ride facing traffic (on the "wrong" side of the street). This keeps your dog as far as possible from cars. Unbelievable as it sounds, some sadistic people will try to hit a dog on a leash while attached to a bike or as you walk him if the dog is on the side next to traffic. (They will not try to hit you because the penalties are too great.) By riding facing traffic, you have a chance to pull off to the very edge of the street or the sidewalk if a car is coming that doesn't allow you a safe amount of room to pass. Watch out for cars pulling out of driveways as you pass; they may not see you.

Never let your dog roam free. Even the best-trained dog can stray from home. Today there are too many dangers, cars especially, that can kill your dog. Even if your dog is perfectly trained off-lead (see "Come!"), stay with him when he is off-lead. Do not let him use his own judgment unattended; he may get hit by a car. No matter how foolish it is, there are still people who let their dogs out alone and who tell you about it proudly. For every such case, there are dozens of dogs who die in the paths of cars. The risk isn't worth it.

CHEWING (ON YOUR HANDS OR CLOTHING)

Chewing on hands or clothing is not really a problem, but many people misunderstand it, and some are disconcerted or even frightened. In any case, chewing can be annoying, so here is the way to teach your puppy or dog to stop doing it.

Many dogs, especially puppies, will chew on your hands or clothing when you are patting them, when they want to get your attention, or simply whenever they are near you. Some breeds, notably bull-dog breeds and boxers, especially like to use their mouths almost as hands. They like to pull your clothing and hang onto it, having a tug-of-war with it.

When a dog puts your hand or clothing into his mouth, he is actually paying you a compliment. He will not do this in a friendly playful way (even though play gets fairly enthusiastic at times!) unless he likes and trusts you.

But if he becomes a nuisance by too much of this playful expression, place your first two fingers, palm down, on the dog's tongue, and push them far enough back to cause the gag reaction. When this happens, the dog coughs or makes a gagging sound and immediately will spit your fingers out of his mouth. Say "Hey!" as you do this correction, so that eventually the dog will learn to stop the behavior for the word alone.

As soon as he has let go of your hand, praise him calmly. If he tries to mouth or bite at your hand again, repeat the correction.

If the dog grabs hold of your clothing and begins to pull it, you may not be able to use this correction because his jaws will probably be closed fairly well. In this case, use the flat of your hand and smack him flat on the top of his head, between his ears. Don't be afraid to slap fairly hard; it must be hard enough so it is unpleasant for him and so he does not think it is simply a new dimension to his already ongoing game of tug-of-war with your clothing. You will know you have done it right if the dog stops; otherwise, repeat, but harder. As usual, say "Hey!" as you give the correction.

Nibbling or chewing puppies or young dogs can frighten small children. (Up to about two years, dogs are themselves still "children" or "adolescents.") Limit the opportunities for your puppy or dog to be with small children. Allow them to be together only when you can supervise them. Correct, as above, as needed.

Often a dog you have rescued from a pound or other frightening or abusive situation will be very subdued for the first week or month, or even longer. Then, when he begins to feel safe with you at last, and decides he loves you and wants never to leave you again, he will become exuberant and joyful. This joy can be expressed in biting on your hands and clothing. It is a sign that you have done a fine job so far in rehabilitating a "lost" dog. If the behavior is too rough (such a dog may never have learned to play and, due to lack of early socialization, may not know how much is "enough"), you need to teach him gently but firmly that you do not like this behavior, but you still love him. Correct him, then give him reassuring pats, body hugs, and talk reassuringly to him.

Note: The more obedience training you give to your dog, the more he will behave himself in other areas of behavior, such as chewing on your hands and clothing. See also "Come!" "Down!" "Heel!" and "Sit!" Obedience training gives your dog positive things to think about, and he will have less time to invent games like chewing on you and your clothing as a result.

CHEWING (ON RUGS, FURNITURE, ETC.)

Almost every young dog chews up almost everything in sight. This is one of the characteristics of puppies everywhere. Luckily it usually tapers off and disappears at about the age of two, when a dog reaches his full maturity. You may wonder why a large dog of a year or a year and a half is still chewing up the floors and walls, or the chairs and bedspreads, when he looks full grown. The answer is that, like a teenage person, he is still a "kid" and not really full-grown mentally until he is two or more.

Prevention is the best solution to chewing. If you have a room where your dog can inflict minimal damage, leave him there when you go out. An even better solution is to crate train your dog. (See "Crates.")

If he manages, despite your efforts, to chew something you care about—a rug or clothing or a piece of furniture—correct him for the wrong action. Take him by the scruff of the neck, drag him over to the chewed item, say loudly "Bad dog!" three or four times, and as you do, swat his thigh with the flat of your hand or, in the case of a big dog, with a jumping bat. (See "Jumping Bat.")

However, do not expect this correction to have any lasting value. Your young dog or puppy will feel *terribly sorry,* right then, that he has upset you. But the next time he is left to his own devices in the presence of some tempting and chewable object, he will not think twice about chewing it up.

If you crate your dog, keep chewable toys in the crate with him. Play with these same toys when you have him out of the crate after you get home. Good toys include a *hard rubber* ball —be sure it is big enough so there is no way he can swallow it— available at pet stores. *Rawhide chew-toys* can be chewed up and swallowed; limit the number of rawhide toys you give your dog so he doesn't eat more than a small piece a week. (No one I have asked seems to know exactly how these toys are "cured" or preserved; many originate in foreign countries where regulations for cleanliness and use of chemicals may be a great deal less stringent than in this country.) Another toy that dogs find irresistible is *cow hooves,* dried and available at pet supply stores. They are so tough that a dog can chew for days and not get completely through one. The only drawback is that they smell when wet. (Dogs think the smell is delicious, but you may have a different opinion.) However if you keep these toys strictly in the crate, and not on your rugs, your dog will have a good reason to like being in his crate, and you will at least confine the smell to one small area.

When you let your dog out into the house, keep an eye on him. If he begins sniffing around a piece of furniture, a pillow, or other nontoy, yell "Hey!" at him and give him a swat on the thigh with your hand. Do this hard enough so he will not think you are playing a game. Eternal vigilance is the price of puppies. Keep your mind on the future; almost all dogs stop chewing, finally, after they grow up.

CHOCOLATE: POISONOUS TO DOGS

Chocolate is highly toxic to your dog. It contains theobromine, which is poisonous to dogs. In sufficient quantities, chocolate can be fatal. Even a small bar of chocolate can make an average-size dog extremely sick.

Be sure never to leave chocolate around the house where a dog or puppy can get at it, and remove leftover chocolate ice cream, chocolate cake, or chocolate cake frosting from areas accessible to the dog.

CLOTHING FOR DOGS

Dogs with very short hair, such as Staffordshire terriers, American pit bull terriers, and Chihuahuas, suffer from the cold and can be real cowards about it. If you live in a climate where it snows or sleets, you may want to try a dog coat for your dog.

Dog coats should fit in the same way your own coat fits you: fairly snugly but not tight. Measure from your dog's neck at the top of the collar straight to the point at which his tail joins his back. You can then order a coat from a mail order catalog or buy one from a pet supply store. If possible, take your dog into the store and try out the coat on him prior to purchase.

Dog coats come in myriad styles and colors. I think the plainer the better, but it doesn't matter as long as you and your dog are happy.

Occasionally a dog is truly embarrassed by having to wear a coat. Some will even hide when it is time to go out, dreading having to wear something they think makes them look ridiculous. If your dog is plainly unhappy, try walking him with another dog in a coat a few times. If even this fails to convince him that wearing a coat is okay, then discontinue using it. Dogs have feelings too, and if your pet prefers to be cold to looking silly, who is to say he's wrong? Just keep him moving a little faster. On the other hand, some dogs think they look quite fancy in their dog coats and will prance along happily, comfortable and warm.

Never put a dog into a crate with any article of clothing on him; he can get hung up and hurt if it catches on one of the many protruding wires that hold the crate together.

Winter Coats for Dogs
*Some dogs think they look really handsome in their winter clothes
and are pleased and proud to wear them.*

COLLARS

There are several different kinds of collars. Each has special purposes, advantages, and disadvantages.

CHOKE CHAIN COLLAR

A choke chain collar, also called a choker, consists of a length of small-link chain, usually with a chrome finish, and a ring approximately three-quarters of an inch or larger at each end. By dropping the chain through one of these rings, you create a collar. When a leash is attached to the other ring, the collar will tighten when you pull. This is the standard collar for training. You cannot train a dog easily—some would say you cannot train properly—without this piece of equipment.

When you pull on the leash, you momentarily cause the collar to tighten. "Choker" is really not an accurate description of the collar, because it does not choke the dog. It merely makes him feel a sharp pull for a moment. As soon as you cease to pull on the leash, the collar immediately loosens up again. It is therefore highly effective in training; it causes discomfort only when the dog does something he isn't supposed to (pulls) and gives no signal to him when he does what he is supposed to (doesn't pull). The collar should just fit over the dog's head with as little slack chain left over as possible. The smaller the links of the chain, the more easily it will slide and release after it has been pulled.

It is extremely important that the choke collar be worn *only*

Types of Collars

Upper left: Cloth Webbing Collar
Center: Prong or Pinch Collar
Upper Right: Choke Chain Training Collar
Lower Right: Rolled Leather Collar

during actual training sessions. The rest of the time it must be removed, or it can become dangerous or even fatal. A dog who wears a choke collar while playing with another dog can be choked to death if the second dog's bottom canine (long) teeth get caught beneath the collar during play, and that dog then lies down and rolls over. This happened in my own living room with two of my dogs, very quickly and without warning. (Should this happen, take the dog whose teeth are caught, by the hind legs, and roll him over to loosen the collar, then help him disengage his teeth.)

The other major danger with a choke collar is when the dog is in his crate. The collar can catch on one of the many hooks protruding inside the crate and choke the dog to death. There are many such documented cases. When you put your dog in a crate, remove *all* collars.

The simplest way to remember is simply to remove the choke collar as soon as you have finished a training session.

WEBBING COLLAR

Webbing collars are made of cloth webbing, sometimes of nylon or a similar tough synthetic. These may be of a single thickness or, for big dogs, double or triple thickness. Dogs should wear this collar at all times *except* in a crate. Keep identification tags (see "Identification Tags and Tattooing") and rabies vaccination tag on this collar.

ROLLED LEATHER COLLAR

Like the webbing collar, a rolled leather collar can be a slightly fancier solution to the problem of keeping identification on your dog at all times. Leather is "rolled" around a piece of rope, which makes it almost impossible for the collar to twist and choke when two dogs are playing together. It is therefore a relatively safe collar. However, remove even this type of collar before leaving a dog in a crate.

FLAT LEATHER COLLAR

Flat leather collars perform the same function as rolled leather collars. The wider the leather strip, the less chance of another dog's turning over with his teeth caught in it and choking your dog.

PRONG COLLAR

A prong collar (sometimes called a pinch collar) is strictly a training device for dogs who pull relentlessly. It is used in place of a choke collar until the problem is corrected. I recommend you try to work with a simple choke collar first, using instructions in the section entitled "Heel!" teaching your dog not to pull on a leash. If you absolutely cannot make a pulling dog heel even using this information, a prong collar may help. Do *not* use the prong collar when longeing. (See p. 109.) It can break the hyoid bone in the dog's neck.

A prong collar consists of a series of links, each about one inch long. Two blunt prongs half an inch long protrude inward from each link. A ring for attachment of the leash allows the collar to be used much as a regular choke collar, but the prongs provide a sharper correction.

The prong collar is adjusted to fit the dog by removing one or more links until the size is snug enough to allow no slack, but not so tight as to cause the prongs to take effect unless the ring is pulled.

Note: When you use a prong collar, attach a second leash to a regular choke collar at the same time. Prong collars sometimes come apart for no reason, and you could otherwise be left without any collar on or control of your dog.

VERY IMPORTANT!

A collar should fit snugly but should never be tight around the dog's neck. As a young dog or puppy grows and develops, it is necessary to remove outgrown collars and replace them with larger ones. The same is true for a dog who was in a poor, skinny condition, and develops muscle and body size with proper care. Failure to remove a too-small collar causes dogs to panic and can lead to what seems to be erratic behavior. It isn't; the dog is simply unable to breathe and panics as a result. (Try it on yourself; you'll be surprised how quickly you feel panic).

If you find or adopt a dog with a too-tight collar, and you find it so tight that you cannot remove it, see a veterinarian without delay; the vet may have to sedate or anesthetize the dog and cut off the collar.

COME! (COME WHEN CALLED)

Coming when called may be the most important command your dog will ever learn. You should teach this essential command as soon as your dog is three months old or older. It is never too late to train a dog to come. *He must come every time you call him, under any and all circumstances.* There are no exceptions to this.

Many people use the command word "Come!" I advise the word "Here!" because it is a crisper, clearer word, and it will carry a long distance when necessary. Make your own choice, but be consistent in its use.

To begin to teach your dog to come, put him on a fifteen-foot-long piece of clothesline rope with a snap on one end and a handle tied on the other. This is called a *longe line* (pronounced "lunge"). Attach the snap to the choker collar so the collar will tighten when you pull on it, just as you would attach a leash. Take the dog outside, and let him wander for a few minutes wherever he likes without telling him anything, just holding onto the end of the longe line as he does so. Then call sharply "Here!" (I use a rather high, flat tone that is clearly a command and not my usual speaking voice.) Keep repeating the command at one-second intervals the entire time you are doing the exercise.

As you call the command, haul the dog toward you, hand over hand on the longe, until he is sitting squarely in front

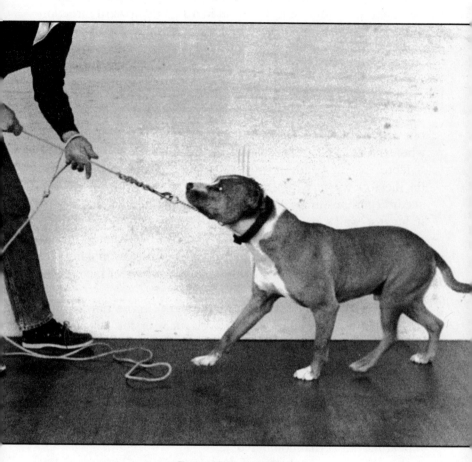

Come When Called
Using the 15-foot longe line attached to the dog's choker collar, haul him toward you. Say the verbal command "Here!" over and over as you pull him toward you.

facing you. If he fails to sit or to sit squarely, grasp each side of his collar and pull him toward you in a slightly upward direction until he is sitting squarely. If necessary, push down on his rear end with one hand. When he is seated properly, praise him, give him a few hugs, and repeat the exercise.

Smart dogs will learn quickly that you are planning to haul them to you and will stay close by, making it difficult to repeat the exercise. If this happens, get an assistant to hold the dog at one end of the longe while you get as far away as possible, and when the assistant releases the dog, repeat.

Note: You can gain in your training almost effortlessly if you do the following: Whenever the dog comes to you of his own accord (perhaps in the house when he knows dinner is ready, or if he just walks up to you for his own reasons), you should repeat the command "Here!" just as if you had wanted him to come to you. In this way you reinforce his action by making him associate it with the verbal command. Make him sit facing you, as just described.

For two weeks, repeat this exercise two or more times a day, for ten consecutive commands. (Each such session will take no more than five minutes.) If you can do three, four, or even five short sessions per day, you will increase your dog's response dramatically. Be sure not to exceed the five-minute limit for each session. Each time your dog responds correctly (even though you may have hauled him to you like a fish) by arriving where you are standing, give him a lot of praise and hugs, while repeating the verbal command.

When the two weeks are over, take your dog to a fenced-in area where you can leave him off lead. Then repeat the exercise. But now, when he thoroughly understands the command, if he fails to obey promptly, catch him and give him a good sharp swat on the thigh with the jumping bat. (See "Jumping Bat.") If you have difficulty catching the dog, replace the longe line with a very light line, made from 1000-pound test fishing line, available in hardware stores, that the dog will not realize is there. Wear gloves; the line can cut your hands when you pull it, especially with a dog who makes a game of running out of your reach. When you have administered the correction with a jumping bat, immediately repeat the exercise, and praise as usual.

Also make a *throw-chain.* Buy a length of metal chain three feet long. For a medium size dog the links of the chain should be about half or three quarters of an inch long, like those used to hang children's swings. For a small dog, use an appropriately shorter, smaller, lighter chain. Wind the chain into a ball, and secure it with string or wire (be sure to bend any wire ends so they cannot be felt when you handle the ball). When you have called your dog and he blithely ignores your command and runs away from you, throw the ball at his feet. If you are able to hit his feet, it will sting (but not harm him at all). Then quickly grab him by the collar, pull him toward you, and repeat the command "Here!" four or five times in a row. Then praise the dog.

Repeat the work daily, several times a day if possible, until your dog obeys every time without hesitation. Have him come straight to you and sit in front of you.

When he does this flawlessly, take the dog, on the fishing line leash, to unfenced areas with distractions such as cows, horses, other dogs, or lots of people and activity such as a schoolyard. Command him to come to you, and find out how well he will respond in the face of many distractions.

Never let your dog off a leash until you are 100 percent sure he will obey you *every time.* Many people do not heed this advice; many, many dogs die each year due to the stupidity of their owners in letting them off lead before they are truly trained.

COPROPHAGY (FECES EATING)

There are many theories on why some dogs eat feces—their own or those of other dogs—none of them conclusive. If your dog gets enough vitamins and minerals, which he will if you feed a good dog food, he probably just developed this unpleasant habit in much the same way people learn to chew their fingernails. It is natural for a bitch to eat the feces of her newborn puppies; the habit may have its roots in a perversion of this.

The best solution is prevention. When a dog leaves droppings, pick them up with a shovel or plastic bag or scooper, and put them into a garbage pail reserved for the purpose. Don't allow a dog with a known taste for feces to be left where he can find them.

Pouring pepper, spraying Bitter Apple (a bad-smelling liquid available at pet stores), or other tactics rarely work, although you can try them.

Sometimes a dog kept away from temptation long enough learns new patterns of behavior and quits the practice on his own.

COPULATING WITH OTHER DOGS

As long as your dog is spayed or neutered, no harm will come of dogs jumping on each other in play and attempting to mate. To dogs this is just a natural part of life, and most will play biting games for a while, go through some of the motions of mating for a few moments, then return to biting and chasing each other.

Dogs will sort out among themselves who is allowed to jump on whom; it depends on their hierarchy. Unless one dog is clearly being persecuted by another dog, there is no need to separate them. The dominant dog jumps the dog(s) below him or her on the hierarchy, regardless of gender.

Play is so good for dogs, both physically and mentally, that it is unkind to prevent their playing together, copulation and all, simply because it may make some human beings uncomfortable.

You may want to make a rule that you allow play of this kind outside in a fenced yard, but not in your living room (where your uncle may be having tea). In that case, make the rule to include *all* roughhousing indoors. If your dogs begin playing inside, take them outside at once. If they must stay indoors in bad weather, separate them. If they begin to play indoors before you can separate them, say "Hey!" sharply, and with the flat of your hand slap each dog on the top of the head hard enough to break his concentration and make him stop playing.

Note: Dogs sometimes also attempt to mount people's legs. A sharp smack on top of the dog's head, and the word "OFF!" corrects this.

CRATES

There are two kinds of dog crates. The first is a wire cage, big enough for the dog to stand, sit, lie down, and move around in without being cramped. His head, when in normal position, should be two or three inches or more from the top of the crate. This crate has a wire grate door that opens outward on one end. The second kind of crate is made of preformed plastic or molded synthetic material, with a wire grate door in front. Two or more small windows are placed high up on the sides and back of the crate. This solid-sided type is often referred to as an "airline crate" as it is standard in shipping dogs on airlines.

Crates can make many dog training problems much easier to solve, and I recommend using them in most cases. A dog who has been properly introduced to his crate considers it his own private room, and many dogs will go into their crates of their own volition when they want to nap or just be left alone for a while. A dog can be left in a crate while the owner is away during the day. I recommend crates for dogs who are destructive, very shy or traumatized, or unhousebroken, or where two or more dogs may fight if left together unattended.

In most cases, a wire crate, which gives the dog the best view of his surroundings, is my choice for dogs. But some dogs are frightened in wire crates although not in those with solid sides. If your dog shows signs of panic in a wire crate, try a solid-sided one.

Important: Always remove all collars and other equipment from the dog before putting him in his crate. He can get caught by the collar and panic, literally choking himself to death.

CURBING

Cities often require that you *curb* your dog. This means making your dog stay off the sidewalks when he defecates, even though you pick the waste up with a plastic bag or scooper. It also means that you have your dog urinate into the edge of the street rather than on the sidewalk. In crowded places where many people must use the sidewalks, there is merit in the ordinance.

Crates
Left: Wire Crate
Right: Solid-Side "Airline" Crate

There is also danger: Cars parking or pulling out from a parking space without warning can hit a dog, even one just doing his business on a leash. It therefore makes good sense to train your dog to use the very outside edge of the sidewalk, still technically the curb, rather than allowing him to step off the sidewalk entirely and stand in the street.

The way to train your dog is through repetition. When he is ready to get down to business, make sure he is standing where you want him. Do this by pushing or placing him gently at the edge of the curb. If he makes a mistake, do not correct him; it is too late. Just wait for the next opportunity, and place him properly.

Note: Bent wire around trees and flowers can damage your dog's eyes. This problem occurs almost exclusively in cities, where people have installed low wire fences around the base of trees along the sidewalks in order to keep dogs from urinating on the trees or flowers. Loose wires at the level of your dog's eyes can scratch his cornea, necessitating costly veterinarian care and possibly damaging your dog's eye permanently. If you live in a city, it is only considerate not to let your dog urinate on these tiny gardens in any case.

Train your dog to stand on the edge of the sidewalk and use the curb as his bathroom.

CUTS AND SCRATCHES

If a cut or scratch is anything more than superficial, you should get your dog antibiotic treatment at your veterinarian's. This is especially important if it is a puncture wound; if it is from a nail, wire, or glass; or if the wound is bleeding profusely.

If the cut is superficial and not deep, pour a small amount of hydrogen peroxide, available over-the-counter at drugstores, into the wound. If your dog shows any tendency to hostility or fear, put a muzzle on him first, and speak soothingly to him as you work on the cut.

It does no good to put salve or Vaseline on a small cut; your dog will lick it off. While it does no harm for a dog to lick a minor cut or abrasion, if the injury does require medication or stitches, it will be necessary to prevent the dog's licking off the medicine or pulling out the stitches.

An Elizabethan collar—sometimes called a "lampshade" because of its shape (a cone-shaped piece of sheet plastic, which fits around the dog's neck and prevents his mouth coming in contact with any part of his body), prevents your dog's licking the cut for as long as he wears the collar. Veterinarians sell them.

Keep an eye on any cut for a few days; if it shows any signs of festering, pus, or excessive swelling (any cut or scrape may swell slightly for a few days), see your vet.

DEATH OF A DOG: WHAT TO DO

Dogs, sadly, in general do not live as long as their human families. Likely you will have to face the death of your pet.

Many people feel they should have a dog killed (usually euphemistically called "put to sleep") when it is old, infirm, or sick.

If you do this, a veterinarian will kill your dog for you. But there is another way to handle the death of your pet. It may or may not be your eventual choice. In our family, we have found that dogs allowed to live their entire lives, with the best health we can give them, choose themselves the time to pass along back into the universe. My own belief is that this is better, because the dog has more control over his own life, lives as many days as nature will allow, and has time to adjust to the next step.

A dog allowed to die naturally, at home, should be made comfortable on a bed that can be washed easily. (A pile of old towels is good.) If he is incontinent, newspapers spread on the floor, thick enough so you can just remove the top layers as they get soiled, will help. Be sure he has water and food if he can eat it. (You may have to feed him by hand.)

The most important thing you can do is sit beside your dog and spend time with him. Just the feel of your body leaning gently against his will comfort a dog. If he is in pain, he may not enjoy being patted. But the feel of your hand against his side or next to his muzzle tells him you care about him.

We had a big yellow dog who had learned a great many tricks. He had been able to beg, catch food off his nose, roll over, crawl, and climb ladders. When he got cancer, he became weaker and weaker, to the point where he could not stand up. He lay on his bed in a part of the house where he could see the family come and go past him during the day. He had always been an exuberant dog; now he was very quiet. Yet he was alert and, in the pragmatic way of all dogs, made the most of the days he had left. He looked so sad one day that we went over to him and said, "Roll over, Sir! Roll over!" He looked up in disbelief, as if to say "How can you think I can roll over when I can't even stand up?" Then he realized the joke and, for the first time in a week, wagged his tail. He died a few hours later. I believe he preferred this end to having a vet stick a needle into his leg.

No dog I have ever observed firsthand, even very sick ones at the end of life, would, I believe, ask for death from you instead of life. Dogs are practical; they make the best of whatever they are handed. As long as a dog can eat or drink, he wants to continue his life, diminished though it may be. Even when he ceases to eat and drink, I believe a dog wants to die on his own terms, to make the decision about this important last act himself.

What a dog wants and needs is comfort and reassurance: Your calm presence, the gentle pressure of your hand, your voice telling him that he won't be forgotten, that his life has mattered to you, that *he matters*. A dog deserves the right to come to the end of his own life and is perfectly capable of doing so without your intervention.

Killing your dog "humanely," "putting him to sleep," makes a neater package of his life, to be sure. Euthanasia is, we're told, "kinder," and we hear of "quality of life" and other terms suggesting that a life sadly diminished should be ended, by us, for our dog's sake. People often prefer this because in a situation where there is really no good solution, they feel, by taking *some* action, a little more in charge of things.

Dogs, I am convinced, see the question differently from most human beings. The experience of dying is owed to every dog, as it has belonged to millions and millions of generations of dogs who preceded this one. Making the choice for euthanasia fails to consider how the *dog* feels about it.

I am against shortening a dog's life for almost any reason, and am for giving him his only chance to live and die on his own terms, without interference, comforted and loved by his human friends to the very end. Every person must, of course, make his or her own decision.

If you have a garden or yard, dig a grave and bury your dog there. If you live in a city this may not be possible; there are pet cemeteries, listed in the Yellow Pages. Some people choose to have their pet's body cremated, and scatter the ashes in a place where the dog was particularly happy.

DEPRESSION

Dogs can get depressed, just as people can. A dog who is depressed probably will not eat, or will only eat sporadically and little. His tail will be down or tucked between his legs. His ears will droop or be partway down against his head. His general demeanor will be sad, quiet, unresponsive.

The first thing to suspect is illness. A dog with internal pain will act depressed. Have a veterinarian check him thoroughly if depression lasts more than a few days. Certain chronic conditions, many of them treatable with medications or acupuncture, can cause depression.

A dog also can show depression when his favorite person is away for a few days. If this is the case, just speak cheerfully to the dog and don't make too much of it.

Small puppies, taken from their littermates and mother, often feel depressed. They may howl or bark at night. Put a hot water bottle wrapped in a towel and a small ticking alarm clock wrapped in a towel in the box with a young puppy, to simulate the conditions he is used to. Comfort a depressed dog or puppy, don't scold him. Distractions, such as a walk or something the dog especially likes to eat, may help take his mind off his sadness. A gentle body hug can reassure and comfort a depressed dog.

DIARRHEA

Diarrhea can be caused by a number of things, some serious and some not serious. If your dog gets diarrhea from eating some food he is unaccustomed to (such as rawhide chew-toys) or if he returns from a boarding kennel with diarrhea, the cause is probably merely change of diet or stress, and will right itself in a few days. Meanwhile, get Pepto-Bismol tablets. For a dog of about fifty pounds, give two tablets at a time. Most dogs will eat them if disguised in cream cheese or meat. If not, open your dog's jaws with your hand and push the tablets as far down his throat as you can, then close his jaws and hold his nose up in the air as you stroke the outside of his throat until he swallows. Give two tablets (less for smaller dogs, more for huge ones) each time the dog has a liquid or very soft bowel movement.

Extreme diarrhea can be a sign of a serious problem, such as worms or a bone stuck in the intestine. If diarrhea is bloody or persists for more than a day or two, or if the dog seems listless or in distress or vomits, don't wait; see a vet at once.

Diarrhea accidents can be cleaned up without a trace by using Nature's Miracle, a stain and odor remover available at some pet stores and veterinarians' offices.

DIGGING HOLES

Most dogs like to dig holes in the ground. It is a form of play, and they enjoy the exercise it gives their muscles. They can't see any good reason why your flower bed, with all that nice soft predug dirt, should be off limits. It seems almost as if they are trying to be naughty, but they are simply inventing a game with the materials at hand (or paw). If you have a yard that is reserved strictly for dogs with a fence buried at least half a foot below ground level, it will do no harm for your dog to dig holes. Just fill them in from time to time so you won't trip when cleaning the yard.

If you want to train your dog not to dig holes, try one of the following methods:

- If you catch your dog in the act, shoot a stream of water from a garden hose at him as you yell loudly "Hey!" You could also use a high-powered water pistol, available at toy stores. Or simply fill a tin can with water and throw the water at him.
- Throw a bomber snap on the ground near the dog and yell "Hey!" at the same time, if you catch him in the act of digging. (See "Aggression with People.")
- If you cannot catch your dog in the act of digging, put a choke collar and leash on him and drag him forcibly to the already dug hole. Yell "Hey!" and throw a bomber snap in the hole.

DISOBEDIENCE:
FAILURE TO OBEY PROMPTLY OR AT ALL

If you give your dog a command, he must obey it within two seconds. If he does not, he is either ignoring you or does not understand what the command means.

If your dog sometimes obeys a command but at other times

does not, he is simply ignoring you. This may occur when he finds something more interesting to pay attention to or when he is distracted. In this case, you must correct him.

If you have given a command that has been disregarded, give the command verbally a second time, using exactly the same tone of voice. At the same time as you repeat the voice command, make the dog physically do what you have commanded. For instance, if you told him to sit, place him in sit position. (See "Sit!") If he again ignores your command, *you must make it worth his while to choose to obey you.* On the second correction for a disregarded command, first swat the dog sharply with the flat of your palm on his thigh, hard enough to sting, and then immediately repeat the voice command, accompanied by the physical positioning of the dog in sit position. This tells him that there will be a penalty for ignoring you.

If you even *think* the dog may not fully understand the command, however, do not use any physical coercion. Instead, go back to the *step before* in training. For instance, if the dog does not fully understand the command for sit, pull up on his collar while pushing down on his hind end in order to teach him the command.

DISHES FOR DOGS

Use stainless steel dishes, not plastic. Plastic gets small scrapes that can harbor bacteria. Stainless steel won't chip or scrape and can be kept spotlessly clean. Periodically pour boiling water into a stainless steel dish to sterilize it.

You can buy little wire devices that hold the dish in place while your dog eats. Some dogs like them, but some, such as

Labrador retrievers, like to carry their bowls around after they finish eating (and sometimes before eating, to remind you that it's time for another square meal), which they cannot do if the dish is placed in a dish holder.

Keep fresh cold tapwater (not from the refrigerator; it is too cold) in a large dish. Change it once or twice a day, especially in summer when extra drinking causes saliva to collect in the water.

DOG FOOD

There are two ways to feed your dog: free feeding, in which food is available at all times and the dog eats as much as he wishes whenever he wishes, and mealtime feeding, in which you feed once or more times a day. Depending on several circumstances, you may choose one or the other method. The method you choose will influence the type of food you feed.

In free feeding, feed dry food only. Moist (canned) food can spoil easily, especially in warm weather. When you choose a dry dog food, sometimes called *kibble*, find one with no red coloring in it. Certain red food colorings have been banned from human consumption. Red dye #2, once commonly used in food for human beings, has been proved to cause cancer. This and other banned dyes are cheap and available for dog foods. Avoid any dog food that lists dyes—usually red, yellow, and sometimes blue. If you can see that the dog food is red in color, reject it.

Some dog food manufacturers have taken to heart the desire of dog owners to provide safe and nutritious food for their pets. They have reduced the number of preservatives in their products, eliminated dyes, and consulted with veterinarians for the most useful combinations of vitamins and supplements.

Listing brand names isn't foolproof, because policy within a company can change radically almost overnight. Companies can be taken over by entirely new ownership, with sometimes disastrous results (for the dogs). However, some of the brands that, at this writing, are generally considered good include Cornucopia, Eukanuba, Iams, and Science Diet. Others, such as KD, are available only through veterinarians. Purina Dog Chow is a low-cost dye-free kibble.

If you choose to feed your dog canned dog food, choose one that provides starch, such as soybean meal, as well as meat. Pure beef, chicken, or horsemeat is not a balanced diet. You may want to mix a few spoonsful of meat with some dry kibble and moisten it with warm water; most dogs like this combination.

If you are teaching a fear-biter (see "Biting Human Beings") to be more trusting of people, feed small amounts by hand several times a day. Use whatever combination of foods is most tempting, as a frightened dog may have little appetite.

If your dog is old or shows signs of health problems, such as kidney failure (a veterinarian can tell you this), follow the vet's advice as to diet.

If you feed at specified mealtimes, allow the dog a quiet few minutes to eat unmolested by other pets, children, or undue activity. When he seems finished, remove any leftover food promptly and store it in the refrigerator until the next feeding. Be sure to warm it slightly with hot water when you next feed it; do not give your dog chilled food directly from the refrigerator.

You can feed once a day or twice a day, or even oftener. Be sure that the total amount of food does not exceed the amount he needs for good health. In general, lean dogs are healthier than chubby ones. If your dog has a padding of fat over his ribs, cut back on the amount you feed.

Food is one of the most important things in a dog's life. Food *matters* a great deal to a dog; he cares far more about it than most people do. Food represents the high point of the day (along with walks), and it is therefore a kindness to your dog to take this interest seriously: give him the best food you can, at regular feeding times or in a free-feeding plan, and allow him to enjoy his food peacefully and without stress.

See also "Snacks and Treats."

DOGNAPPING

Stealing of dogs, usually for monetary gain, has been around for a long time. Today, with drug addiction a major problem across the country, dognapping has grown far worse. You can *never* safely leave your dog unattended, even for a moment when you go into a store, even in your own fenced yard. All it takes is one drug addict bent on stealing your dog for fast profit.

The U.S. government licenses dog dealers, who then supply hospitals, veterinary teaching hospitals, and dental schools with healthy dogs to be used by students and then killed. Every doctor, dentist, and veterinarian you now patronize learned his trade on living dogs (and cats). The market for dogs is huge and ongoing. (See the box under "Adopting Out a Dog.")

In addition, all drug and pharmaceutical companies buy healthy dogs for their salespeople to use in demonstrating company products such as staple guns (used on operations on the intestine, for instance). A dog is anesthetized, cut open, his stomach stapled, and then, when the salesman is through, killed.

Other horror stories include gun clubs that buy dogs from dealers, tie one or more up on long ropes in a gravel pit, and then use them for target practice. A policewoman I know in New Jersey witnessed this.

Another type of dognapping involves holding the dog for ransom. A dog may be stolen from your fenced backyard, and you receive a telephone call later telling you to mail several hundred or thousands of dollars to a post office box, or leave it in a particular place in an envelope, or you'll never see your dog alive again. Often you will never see your dog again in any case; dognappers care only about getting money, not about "playing fair."

In big cities I have heard of yet another scam for stealing dogs. People with small dogs, such as toy Poodles, Cairn terriers, and other breeds small enough to be carried in one hand, have reported being approached by friendly-seeming strangers who begin to pat their cute little dog, then suddenly unsnap the dog's leash, throw the dog into a shoulder bag, jump into a car, and disappear. These cases are nearly always ransom demands, although small dogs also may be sold to people who fight dogs for money. These people require a steady stream of small dogs and cats to use to train their dogs to kill other animals.

The advice is overwhelmingly strong: *Never* leave to chance the safety and life of your dog. He depends on you. Treat a dog the same way you would a small child of two or three. Even if your own neighborhood is "safe," someone with a car can drive into it and steal a dog as easily there as anywhere else. Realize that this is today's reality, and don't ever give a dognapper a chance to steal a dog.

See also "Identification Tags and Tattooing."

DOG-SITTERS AND DOG-WALKING SERVICES

Dog-sitters are people who come to your house while you are away, and feed and let your dog outside into a fenced yard or put him onto a trolley wire.

Dog-walking services come to your house while you are away and take your dog outside on a walk, usually with several other client dogs at the same time.

The essential quality in both dog-walkers and dog-sitters is that they be responsible and competent. There is nothing so dangerous to your dog as an incompetent dog-walker or dog-sitter.

The best way to find a good service is through word of mouth. Ask at your vet's. When you find a service that sounds good, ask for references of people the service has done work for. Then call the references to ask if the people were pleased with the work and whether they have any reservations. Do not assume someone is competent just because he or she has been in business for a certain number of years.

The advantage of a dog-sitter is that your dog remains in much the usual circumstances during your absence. The familiarity of his home and of the routine (ask a dog-sitter to feed and let out your dog at approximately the same times that you do) will be reassuring to him.

The advantage to a dog-walking service is that your dog gets exercise; in a city there may be no alternative, as most people do not have yards. The disadvantage is that a dog being walked by a stranger can get loose and lost, a serious problem as he may not come back to a stranger when called. For this reason alone, I recommend a dog-sitter over a dog-walking service, as long as both are competent.

If you have *any* doubts about the competence of the service you are considering, do not hire it. Board your dog instead. (See "Boarding Kennels.")

If you do use a service, make the person completely familiar with your routine for feeding and exercise. Leave the choke collar and leash where they are readily accessible. Place dog dishes and food where it is easy to get at. Be sure the service has your door key and make sure the person can use it. (Some doors are easy for the owner to open but difficult for others not familiar with the peculiarities of your locks.)

If possible, get a service where the person you hire is bonded. This means that the person who will be entering your house to look after your dog has put a certain number of thousands of dollars into a special account, against the possibility of anything being stolen or lost from your premises while the service is in your employ. While this does not absolutely guarantee honesty, it usually is a fairly good indication that the service is a good one.

One of the best ways to arrange for dog-sitting is to exchange this service with a dog-owning friend. That way it costs you nothing but a little time, and you have the advantage of already knowing the person who will be entering your house and to whose care your dog's life will be entrusted in your absence.

DOORS: DOUBLE, REVOLVING, ELEVATOR

Double doors present no trouble if you keep your dog in heel position at your left, and open the door with your free hand.

Revolving doors are a hazard for dogs unless you can pick them up and carry them through. If your dog is too big for this, do not take him through a revolving door.

Even if you are able to inch your way through carefully, being sure you don't catch your dog's feet as you go, it still is quite possible another person will come along in a hurry and do the damage.

Elevator doors are safe if you follow one simple rule; they can be deadly if you ignore this rule.

The rule is: *Always* place your hand on the closing edge of the elevator door *before* you allow your dog to step into an open elevator. That way you can prevent the door from closing with you outside the elevator and your dog inside it. If this happens, the elevator can move to another floor with your dog in it, the leash caught in the door and perhaps still on your wrist. Your dog will choke to death, and you also may be hurt. Do not allow your dog to enter the elevator in advance of you. You and your dog should enter at the same time, with your dog in heel position at your left. As you prepare to step into the elevator, place your palm firmly against the open door edge, so that if it begins to shut, your hand will prevent it.

Step *off* the elevator in exactly the same way: Put your hand on the closing edge of the door as it opens, hold it for the entire time you and your dog are getting off, and exit with your dog at your left side in heel position.

DOWN! (LIE DOWN)

Have your dog on a choke collar and leash. Place the dog in heel position (see "Heel!") on your left-hand side.

With your right hand holding the end of the leash straight up in the air, step with your foot onto the leash about six inches from where it attaches to the dog's choke collar.

Step down decisively on top of the leash (the leash should cross under your instep) until your foot reaches the ground.

Down! (Lie Down)
Hold the leash with one hand, and step down decisively on the leash to make the dog lie down.

Then stand with most of your weight on the foot holding the leash to the ground. Keep your right hand, holding the handle of the leash, just high enough in the air so you maintain light tension on the leash. The dog will be pulled downward to the ground.

As you do this, repeat clearly the verbal command "Down!" ten or twenty times in a row. Make sure to let a couple of seconds elapse between each repetition so it is clear that the command consists of just one word.

When the dog has remained on the ground in some semblance of down position (he may sprawl on one side or lie in a sloppy-looking way at first), let him up again. To do this, give the command for heel. Then after you walk a few feet, repeat the exercise.

Note: If the dog refuses to lie down, topple him. (See p. 22.)

EATING FOOD FROM THE STREET

Most dogs, unless taught never to do it, will attempt to pick up and eat food they find on the streets when you walk them.

It is very important to teach your dog never to do this. In addition to spoiled food, poisoned food in and around garbage pails is all too easy for a dog to find and eat. There have been instances, not as infrequent as you might assume, of people deliberately putting out poison with the intention of killing dogs. All it takes is one such encounter to spell the end of your pet.

Teach your dog, when walking at your side in heel position, or when you have said "Okay!" to allow him to make full use of the length of the leash, not to pick up *anything* with his mouth.

The moment your dog attempts to pick up something from the street, pull straight upward on the leash, to lift his front end off the ground so his front paws are several inches from the ground and at the same time pull the food or object, disgusting though it may be, out of his jaws. You may have to open his jaws by placing your hand, palm down, across the bridge of his nose and bending his dewlaps (lip skin) against his teeth, pressing until it hurts enough for him to open his mouth. He will not be able to bite you while you are holding him up in the air. It is essential that you make the experience very unpleasant for him. Hold him up for about six or eight seconds, even though you have removed the food from his jaws and thrown it out of reach. Then let him down, and say loudly "No!" Give a sharp jerk on the leash as you say the command, to emphasize the point.

Again approach the piece of food, but do not get close enough for the dog to grab it. (He may try again.) While you hold him a couple of feet from the object, jerk on his leash once and say "No!" again. If he shows any inclination to go after the object, lift him up again as before, and hold him there for five or six seconds. By the second time, he should have got the message loud and clear: He must never pick up food from the street.

If your dog lowers his ears and flattens them somewhat against his head, he shows he has submitted to your wishes. However, if he still perks his ears up and strains toward the food, he has not accepted your command, and you need to repeat the lesson until he does show submission.

While walking your dog, keep an eye out for possible temptations. Say "No!" *before* you reach the food, and remind the dog with a sharp jerk on the leash before you get close enough for him to pick something up. Then walk past with the dog in heel position.

Note: In towns and suburbia, a different problem related to eating on the street confronts dogs. In spring, dogs eat grass, which mixes with excess stomach acid in their stomachs. Dogs then vomit this, getting rid of the acid.

The danger today is that many property owners spray their grass with poisons that, from the reports of many, many dog owners, has caused a particularly deadly type of cancer. Therefore, do not let your dog eat grass from anyone's lawn. (In fact, do not let your dog even walk on lawns that may have been sprayed.) Lawns that appear particularly lush, green, and uniform (no weeds) are especially suspect.

See the note on chemical lawn sprays in "Household Items That Can Harm Your Dog."

EYES: GUMMY DISCHARGE

A thick gummy discharge from the inside corner of your dog's eyes may be a sign of infection. If you notice such a discharge for more than a day or two, have your dog checked by a veterinarian. Eyes are too important to take chances with, being close to the brain of the dog. Infections of the eye are therefore to be taken seriously, as they can, untreated, lead to infection in the brain.

A gummy discharge may be the result of allergies rather than infection; in this case, your vet may recommend an antihistamine such as Atarex. (Taken in conjunction with Derm Caps, which provide essential fatty acids, Atarex works even better.) Sometimes infected teeth (molars) can cause swelling and/or discharge around the eyes. This, too, is serious and requires immediate veterinary examination.

Prevent your dog from scratching or pawing at his eyes. If they itch or hurt, a prompt visit to the vet is warranted.

FANS

A dog is like a small child. His judgment regarding fans and other household appliances is not reliable. If a dog smells something fascinating blowing into the room through a fan, he may try to go through the fan to get at it.

Keep fans where the dog cannot come into contact with them. This is especially critical if the fan is the old-fashioned kind with wide spaces between the protective bars. Even though newer fans have spaces only half an inch wide, through which most dogs cannot push their noses, these also should be placed where a dog cannot get near them.

Be sure a fan does not blow directly on your dog, particularly if he is confined to a crate.

See also "Air-conditioning and Your Dog."

FEARS:
OVERREACTION TO LOUD NOISE, TRAFFIC, AND THUNDER

If your dog overreacts with fear to loud noises, traffic on the street, new people, and so forth, he has probably been badly frightened or traumatized at some point in his early life. Note: A too-tight collar can make a dog panicky. (His air is being cut off. Be sure you can fit two fingers easily between neck and collar. In extreme cases, a veterinarian may be needed to help remove a grossly tight collar.)

The best cure for panic reactions to fairly normal daily activities is to acclimatize your dog by exposing him to the situations that frighten him. Be certain that you do so in a very gradual way, however. Too much too soon will make the problem worse, not better.

TRAFFIC

If your dog is afraid of traffic, for example, put two collars (choke collars that fit snugly) and two separate leashes on him. This insures that he will not slip a collar or break a leash in his panic. Be sure he is wearing identification tags on his non-choke collar, which remains on him at all times.

Take the dog on a short walk where there is not much traffic. Let him see by your attitude that you do not pay any attention to either the traffic or his panic. Be matter-of-fact in your manner and in the way you talk to the dog. A brisk "Come along, now!" said in a confident tone of voice tells him you are going to walk forward even if he is acting frightened. If he pulls back, haul him smoothly along with you, whether he likes it or not. When you have gone eight or ten steps, go back again, and take him indoors.

In an hour or two repeat the exercise, going only a few feet from the front door. Over the course of a week, increase the number of steps you take. You probably will have to haul the dog away from your house and hold him back with all your strength when you turn toward home.

Make no attempt to make him heel at this point. You are dealing with panic; the dog cannot engage his mind in obeying a command while he is panic-stricken.

But in a very quiet area, where he will not panic (your living room will do if there is nowhere outdoors that fits the bill), give the dog lessons in heel. (See "Heel! [Longeing].") Teach him this, and use the exercise frequently. It is very helpful with frightened dogs. This will prepare him to pay attention to this needed command as his panic subsides.

Early trauma can never be overcome completely. In an emergency, a traumatized dog will revert, at least for a moment, to the behavior that he learned in response to trauma. But by training and conditioning, you can change his behavior to the point where the dog, after feeling an initial moment of panic, will respond by obeying you.

THUNDER

Note: Some dogs react with sheer terror to thunder. For them summertime is a tense and panic-filled time, and it's not much fun for their owners.

You can do several things to help make the situation more bearable, although none of them is 100 percent effective.

- Because you cannot eliminate the thunder sounds, your only option is to "dilute" them in another way: by adding other sounds. If you play loud music, preferably with a strong percussion beat to it, the thunder will not sound so bad to the dog, because it will not suddenly erupt against a quiet background. Start playing the music before the storm arrives, if possible so the first rolls of thunder are mixed in with the music, which the dog will be used to hearing by that time. This method is not acceptable, however, if your neighbors object.
- Some dogs feel safer during thunderstorms if they are allowed to hide in a closet or under a bed. Let the dog do this. (Be sure you don't accidentally lock him in the closet.)

If he is crate trained, put him in his crate and cover it with a blanket.

- Sit with your dog on his bed, and cover him with a thick quilt or blanket. This will diminish the noise slightly, and it is very comforting to some dogs.

- Veterinarians prescribe Valium or other drugs that calm a dog's jangled nerves to a certain degree. I prefer methods that do not involve drugs, but in some cases drugs work better than anything else. If your dog does not respond to either of the preceding approaches, try your vet next.

- Your own attitude is of major importance. Keep your manner calm, cheerful, matter-of-fact. Your dog takes his cue from you, as pack leader, more than you think. Don't let the dog's panic cause you to overreact or to show him too much concern. By so doing you convince the dog that there is, indeed, something very dangerous going on, since you, his pack leader, are showing so much concern. Comfort your dog as suggested earlier, but don't say or do anything that could make him think that you take his panic, or the noise of thunder, too seriously.

To help a dog who is extremely shy or fears strangers, have him on a leash with a choke collar. Sit down yourself, holding him on a leash only a foot or two in length, so he remains close to you. Have another person the dog does not know approach him, but not come closer than five or six feet. A frightened dog may act with aggression, barking, growling, or raising the fur on his back. Say to him with an authoritative tone, "No, it's all right. *I'm* in charge here, not you," or any other words you like. Your tone matters most. You need to *sound* in charge of the situation. Have the stranger "wag his tail" (tap his hand against his own thigh, in the manner of a dog wagging his tail) but not approach the dog. Slowly and gradually, let your dog approach him instead. The "wagging tail" does much to allay a frightened dog's fears. The stranger should also speak quietly and reassuringly to the dog the whole time. He must *not* extend his hand to the dog, which is a threatening gesture to a frightened animal. Let the dog come to him, as near as he is willing to come. Then quit, praise the dog. Repeat the exercise frequently; repetition is the key.

See "Stress."

FENCES: ELECTRIC OR "INVISIBLE"

Electric or "invisible fences" can work well for some dogs, to keep them from straying off the property. The dog wears a battery-equipped collar that shocks his neck if he crosses the ground under which an electric wire is buried.

Many dogs quickly learn how far toward the road is "safe" for them to go and will run, bark, and play within the allowed area.

Two kinds of dogs should *not* be confined with an invisible fence. Dogs who are terribly frightened and nervous will be made even more so and may finally only cower in one spot. And dogs with enormous egos and a high pain threshold (some of the bull breeds are well known for this; they consider it a sign of macho pride to ignore pain of any kind) will stroll through an invisible fence while the collar gives off its best shocks without effect.

The Yellow Pages in your telephone book list companies that will install invisible fencing. See also "Trolley Wires."

FIGHTS BETWEEN DOGS:
HOW TO BREAK THEM UP

Most dogfights look and sound much worse than they actually turn out to be. Nevertheless, they are extremely unpleasant, and if one begins you should break it up without delay.

Dogs fight one of two ways. Many breeds, including German shepherds, golden retrievers, and cocker spaniels, fight by making lots of noise and biting in slashing bites one after another.

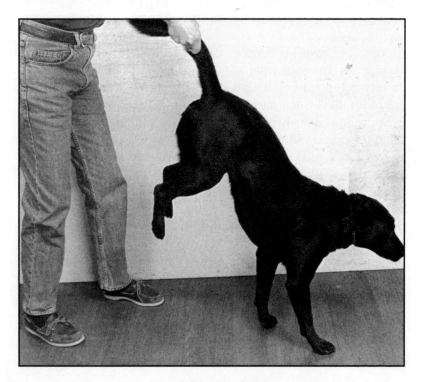

Break Up Dogfights
by pulling the dogs apart by their hind legs or tails.
Lift upward as you pull backward.

With these and a great many other breeds and mixed breeds, you can break up the fight by breaking one dog's hold on the other dog. This can be done sometimes by nothing more than a severe swat on the head with a book. (A thin, large, flat children's book works well.) Another useful method is to dash a glass of hot water into the jaws of the dog who is holding onto the other dog. A third method is to cover the dogs' heads with a blanket or coat, then pull them apart by their tails or hind legs.

The bull breeds, such as Boston bull terriers, English bull-

Pull up and back on hind legs to break up dogfights.
Both owners should act simultaneously.

dogs, bull mastiffs, shar-peis and all terrier breeds, including Jack Russells and Staffordshires, fight in an entirely different way. Their style is to take a good hold on their opponent and then just sit back while the enemy wears himself to a frazzle trying to get loose. Hitting a bull breed on the head is of no use whatever in breaking his hold on the other dog. He won't even notice that you are doing it.

With these dogs, what works best is to put a stick, such as a broom handle, between the dog's jaws and pry them open like a can opener. Then you need to be sure the two dogs cannot grab each other a second time; this may require some fast work if you are alone, and is much easier if there are other people present who understand what must be done. Another method that may work is to cover both dogs' heads with a coat or blanket, then pull them apart by their tails or hind legs.

Here are some other methods of separating two fighting dogs:

- Pick up the dog's hind legs from behind, one in each hand. Raise the legs to your waist height, and pull the dog backward. Note: This will not work with the bull breeds, who will not break their hold unless you pry open their jaws.
- Pick up the dog's tail from behind, raise his body to your waist height, via your hold on the tail, and pull the dog backward. This will not work with the bull breeds until you pry open their jaws.
- If a hose is available, a sudden jet of cold water often can break up a dogfight. If available, a can full of hot water is sometimes effective. Throw it right into the faces of the warring parties.

Never try to separate two dogs by grabbing their collars. In the heat of the moment, one is almost sure to bite you accidentally.

See also "Aggression with Other Dogs."

FLATULENCE (GAS)

If your dog eats something he is not accustomed to (rawhide toys, broccoli, onions), he may exhibit increased gas. In such cases, the problem will cure itself in a day or two.

But if your dog exhibits gas in large or persistent quantities, especially if it is accompanied by vomiting, diarrhea, swollen stomach, or constipation, he may have a malfunction of the digestive system. This can be fatal if left untreated. (See "Bloat.")

Worms, infections, poisons (licking floors or grass where insecticides have been sprayed, for instance), ingestion of foreign materials such as golf balls, rubber toys, metal dog food cans, and the like all can cause digestive malfunction. All require a veterinarian's examination, the sooner the better. Often conditions that are fully treatable at the early stages cause death if allowed to progress without treatment until it is too late.

FLEAS

Fleas exist in most parts of the United States. They are worse in some areas, notably Florida. They seem to become more prevalent at certain times of the year, especially in late summer and fall, and usually diminish or disappear in winter. Fleas cause worms, hair loss, and itchy skin.

There are two types of flea spray: One is for use on the dog himself, and the other is for household use on his bed and in the house. Accidental use of the household spray on a living animal can cause shock and death of the pet.

Ask your veterinarian for a reliable spray to use on your dog and for a spray to use in your house.

Instructions on the bottle will tell you to spray your dog several times a week. I recommend that you do not use it so often. Instead of this, also purchase a *flea comb,* which is a very fine-toothed metal comb. Spray onto the comb rather than onto the dog. Then comb the dog's hair, paying special attention to the area all around his tail, around his ears, under his neck, and anywhere the dog has obviously been scratching. The fine-toothed comb may catch some fleas. (The spray on the comb will get rid of them.) Use the comb as often as you can.

A second treatment, which is a bit more trouble but which has no potentially harmful side effects, is to put your dog into a tub of comfortably warm water, deep enough to cover the entire dog except for his head. Wet his neck and lather it with baby shampoo. Keep the dog standing, submerged except for his head and neck, for five or six minutes. Then lather the dog and rinse. All the fleas on the dog will drop off within this time.

Flea and tick dips are effective, but they are also poisons, and the long-term effects may be harmful. Try not to dip your dog unless he is infested; if you must dip him (a grooming parlor also can do this for you), do it as infrequently as possible.

Flea collars generally do not work as well as you might think from their advertising. Some dogs have severe reactions to them when they get wet. Many people choose to avoid their use entirely. If you get one, use it according to instructions.

Electronic flea collars, which are battery operated, drive fleas away by emitting a noise at frequency disturbing to them but inaudible to human beings or dogs. Some people have reported good success with their use; they are available for about $20 to $30 from pet stores and mail order catalogs specializing in pet supplies. Ask your vet. A small battery is enclosed in a collar, generally made of plastic, which is strapped around the dog's neck in the usual way.

Note: Be sure to spray your house at the same time you treat your dog for fleas. Unless you do so, fleas hiding in rugs or cracks in the floor and in furniture will jump back onto the dog.

Important! Flea spray intended for use on the house itself (rather than for use on pets) must never be sprayed on an animal. To do so will cause shock and will probably cause death. Be sure there are no animals of any kind—dogs, cats, birds, gerbils or hamsters, reptiles, turtles, fish, or anything else that breathes —in the house for at least two hours or more while spraying and after you have finished. Once the spray has dried, veterinarians consider it to be harmless. Follow instructions carefully while using it. You may have to repeat the household treatment two to three weeks after the first application in order to get rid of newly hatched fleas.

See also "Itchy Skin." Many other conditions mimic flea-bite itching, and unless you actually see one or more fleas on your dog when you comb him with a fine-toothed flea comb, you may be treating your dog for fleas when the problem is something else entirely.

FLY BITES

Ordinary houseflies, as well as deer flies and horseflies, can make a dog who lives outdoors suffer terribly. Dogs with cut ears (such as most Doberman pinschers) are especially vulnerable because there is a larger surface without hair along the cut part of the ear. But all dogs can be made miserable by fly bites, especially on the ears, causing scabby or raw areas, itching, pain, and infection.

The solution is extremely simple. Apply insect repellent, the same over-the-counter brands you would use on a human being, daily to the ears, tail, or any other area flies seem to be attacking on the dog. Be sure not to get the fly repellent in the dog's eyes accidentally. If you do, flush liberally with water, and watch for rubbing of the eyes with a paw. If this happens, continue flushing with water or see your vet.

FRENZIED BEHAVIOR

If your dog engages in frenzied running, scooting (running with his tail end lowered, in almost a sitting position), and/or nipping at your hands or clothes, he is playing. This frenzied behavior shows he is confident enough to be really silly in your presence.

It can be a nuisance, however, especially if the dog gets carried away to the point of actually nipping you hard enough to hurt. What he is saying by this behavior is "I'm overjoyed with my life, I love the person I am showing off in front of, I trust him so much I know he will love me if I show him my silliest side, and I think he is good enough to eat, so I'll nibble him while I'm at it."

The best way to discourage overfrenetic behavior is to distract the dog with a game that has some sort of rules. Throw a Frisbee or a ball. (It works even better to have *two* balls or Frisbees, so you are spared the chore of prying the object out of the overactive dog's jaws; just throw the other one.) Also, exercise will help to calm down an overactive dog. (See "Bicycle Riding with Your Dog.")

Don't panic. Frenzied behavior, while you may not exactly welcome it, is actually a compliment to you.

FURNITURE: GETTING UP ON

Dogs can easily be trained not to get up on furniture. It seems to be much harder to train human beings to be consistent about whether the dog is allowed on furniture. If you allow your dog on furniture, or on a particular piece of furniture, you cannot expect him *not* to get on it whenever you change your mind. So the first rule about dogs on furniture is this: Make up your own mind, and be consistent.

If you have decided your dog is never allowed on furniture, wait until you catch him on a couch, chair, or bed, then smack his thigh with the jumping bat. (See "Jumping Bat.")

If you cannot easily catch the dog to give him the correction with the jumping bat, leave a two-foot length of rope tied to his regular (not his choke) collar. Do not use a leash; it will be too long and will snag on objects as he walks around. This length of rope is enough for you to catch the dog easily and to hold him still while you give him a corrective smack with the bat.

As you give the dog a swat with the bat, pull him over to the couch, chair, or wherever he had illegally gotten up on furniture and make it clear that this is the reason for the correction. If you see him on furniture in future, say "Hey!" immediately, and repeat the correction as given.

However, if you let your dogs up on furniture, it can be a nice companionable way to share time. Be consistent if you do.

Allowing Dogs to Get Up on Furniture
can be a companionable way to share time together.
But you must be consistent.

HEATSTROKE

A dog's normal temperature is from 100 to 102 degrees Fahrenheit. A dog unable to escape extreme heat—in a parked car, for example, where the temperature *even with windows left partly open can soar within two minutes to 112 degrees*—can quickly develop heatstroke and die. *Never* leave a dog unattended in a parked car.

A dog left outdoors without access to shade and without sufficient water can also get heatstroke.

A dog with heatstroke will show muscle tremors (twitching, shaking muscles in the legs primarily), may stagger and appear dazed, and may collapse.

Bring down the dog's body temperature with cool water, and get the dog to a veterinarian immediately.

Obviously prevention is the only intelligent solution.

HEEL!:
TEACHING YOUR DOG NOT TO PULL ON A LEASH (LONGEING)

When you walk your dog he should not pull on the leash. He should walk quietly at your left side no matter what length leash you allow him: two feet, four feet, eight feet, or any other length.

Whether your dog pulls forward out of exuberance, backward due to extreme shyness, or sideways, up, or down in response to squirrels that need to be taught a lesson, the most effective single correction is *longeing* (pronounced "lunge-ing").

Longeing is a procedure stunning in its simplicity. It is entirely logical, which is the reason it works well with almost every dog; dogs are the most logical of creatures, very good observers of cause and effect, and highly interested in the subject. Dogs continually study human beings for clues to making them do what the dogs want them to do.

Longeing was invented by William Koehler, whom many of today's top trainers consider to be the best dog trainer this country has ever produced.

The equipment you will need is a regular choke collar (see "Collars") and a ten-foot leash with a safety snap fastened securely to one end. You can make a leash using sash cord (stronger than clothesline rope) and a snap, available at hardware stores. Tie a hand-loop in one end, and tie the snap to the other using six or eight knots so it won't come undone with use.

Go to a field or open area, such as a playground or schoolyard, if possible. Hold the leash handle as shown in the illustration, p. 112. Place your hand on your belt buckle. Your right hand holds the leash handle. *Your two hands lock together, with one over your belt buckle, and never move. This point is essential.* The reason is that it is your body movements, not jerks on the leash, that will signal the dog what you want him to do. Your aim is to teach him to watch your body movements for cues, and then adjust his own position relative to yours.

Without speaking to the dog or giving him any clue that you intend to move forward, begin walking briskly ahead. It is your body movements, not a command, that the dog must learn to pay attention to.

As you move forward, walk purposefully but do not rush. Walk about twenty paces, turn sharply to the right, walk another twenty paces, turn right again, and so on to make a large square, clockwise.

If your dog pulls you in a forward direction as you proceed, turn your body in an about-face by pivoting on your right foot and turning to face the opposite direction and move briskly and decisively forward in this new direction. Remember to keep both hands firmly in place on your belt buckle. Do *not* give in to the temptation many feel to jerk on the leash for good measure. Simply move in the exact opposite of the direction you were going. Your dog will probably continue heading in the old direction. (After all, he had surged forward without any correction from you and thinks he is now the leader of the parade.) He quickly finds out otherwise; instead of being at the front, he now finds himself at the very tail end of the action. The leash will suddenly jerk him after you, and he will have to run to catch up.

Continue walking in the new direction until and unless the dog pulls ahead again. If he does, spin around again and head in the opposite direction. Very quickly (usually within a half hour or so) most dogs will realize that there is no "ahead" direction except as it relates to *you*. And the logical dog then says to himself, "Okay, I get it, I see how it works. What I need to do is keep my eye on this person at all times so he/she can't surprise me by doing an about-face and heading off in the opposite direction." And when your dog does begin to watch you and to position himself near you in order not to have you pull a switch of direction, you have laid down the first and most essential element of teaching your dog to heel.

Because the leash is long, much of it will drag on the ground. This is normal. Other than not tripping on it, don't pay any attention to the extra length of leash. Just remember to keep both hands immovable on your belt buckle at all times.

If your dog stays reasonably near you (either side is all right at first; don't correct him yet for walking on your right) and does *not* pull on the leash, continue to walk on the square, turning right at each corner. Do this ten times, then change direction and make the square to the left (counterclockwise). If you are athletic and fit, you can add a variation; when you are required to do an about-face, instead of walking in the new direction, *run* at full speed instead. This has the effect of chang-

Longeing
Take a secure hold by putting your right hand through the handle of the longe line. Grasp the line just below with your left hand. Then hook your right thumb onto your belt buckle to keep your hands motionless.

ing the amount of time your dog has to adapt to a change of direction and catch up with you. After running once or twice, you probably will find your dog makes an effort to get back to your side more quickly.

A word of caution: If a dog who has never learned to walk on a leash at all (such as some strays about whom you know little or nothing of their history) should actually pull back until he chokes himself and even, possibly, falls over, do *not* merely pull him along. A dog who truly does not understand anything at all about leash work could injure himself or pass out. You will need to proceed slowly with such a dog. Teach him, in a small area, such as a room or small pen with clear size limitations, how to walk along at your left side. Do this by holding him in position

*Close your hands around the longe line
for a secure grip.*

as strongly as necessary but as gently as possible until he understands in general that he is supposed to walk *with* you. Then begin longeing exercises, a week or two later.

However, if a dog clearly understands something about walking on a leash, but due to extreme shyness or fright holds back, pulling you in a backward direction, pull him inexorably along with you. (If he pulls south, you walk—or run—north.)

You can practice walking through obstacle courses while longeing, once your dog gets a general understanding of the procedure. For instance, find two trees about three feet apart. Walk purposefully between them. Your dog will probably at first try to take a short-cut and go outside of the trees. When you have passed between the trees but the dog hasn't, inevitably the dog will suddenly find himself jerked unceremoniously toward the trees and forced to pass between them just as you did. A few tries at this exercise will usually find a dog paying ever closer attention to *exactly where that human being walked,* because this has important consequences for the dog's own comfort. An especially intelligent dog will enjoy the challenge of this "game"; even a not very bright dog will realize that he can control his own comfort (and avoid being jerked along on the leash) if he keeps a close watch on you and goes where you go.

From here is it a short step to stage two: varying the length of leash and repeating the exercises. Proceed to the second stage only after your dog fully understands the first (walking with you on a very long longe line without pulling). Before you move on to stage two, place some tempting distractions around your work area—toys, food, squirrels if you have any—to check your dog's obedience in the face of terrible temptation. If you have done your work correctly, and enough of it, your dog will pass even the most tempting distraction in order to keep an eye on you. When he does so correctly, place him at your left-hand side and allow him only enough leash so he must stay in place next to you.

There are two other ways to teach a dog to heel. Some people may find them useful.

Using a choke collar and four-foot leash, place your dog at your left side in sit position. Put your right hand through the leash handle and grasp the leash just below. Hold your left hand just below your right, on the leash handle. It is important to keep both hands together on the leash handle, as you must use both hands at the same moment as a unit when you give the correction.

Begin by allowing the dog about one to two feet of leash, depending on the dog's size. (A very small dog will require more leash just to reach down to him.) Say "Heel!" in a clear crisp command—don't yell the word, just say it clearly. Start to walk forward with your left foot first, the foot nearest the dog's head, which will cue him that you are moving forward.

If he does not pull, simply walk along repeating the word "Heel!" every few seconds to reinforce the command. But as soon as the dog pulls on the leash, even a little bit, do the following: Continue to hold the handle of the leash with both hands. Bend your knees so that your overall height, without bending your body forward, is about six inches shorter than your normal height. This lowers your center of gravity and puts you in a stronger position to give the correction.

Turn sideways to the dog, so your right foot is ahead of the left foot. Move both hands forward, toward the dog, momentarily creating slack in the leash. Then, as abruptly as you can, jerk the leash toward your body.

Doing this quite sharply will not hurt the dog (except with an old or a frail dog, in which case you should *not* perform this correction). *The key to success is not actually how hard you pull, but rather how abruptly.* The faster and sharper the action, the more successful it will be.

At the same instant that you jerk the leash backward, say in a clear voice the command word "Heel!" Remember not to yell the word; it is the sharpness of the jerk on the leash, not the loudness of the command word, that will change the dog's behavior.

As soon as the dog stops pulling, even for a moment, walk forward as before (left foot first) and behave as if nothing had happened. But be ready for the dog to begin to pull again, and repeat the correction. If you have to repeat it more than five or six times in a row, you are not jerking the leash quickly enough or hard enough, or both.

Very big dogs, such as a shepherds, mastiffs, great Danes, and golden retrievers, or very stubborn dogs, such as some terriers, may continue to pull despite your giving the correction correctly. In this case, use a prong collar (see illustration, p. 64) for a few sessions. (The dog will learn that you have this quite unpleasant tool at your command and will decide that it is less trouble to heel than to have you use the prong collar on him.) A prong collar consists of adjustable links with metal prongs turned inward that poke the neck of the dog when he pulls. They are sold in pet supply stores.

Adjust the prong collar so it fits comfortably but not loosely, with the prongs turned inward. Attach the leash to the round

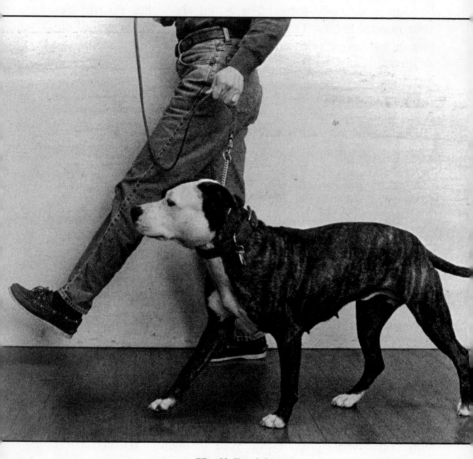

Heel! Position
Start to walk forward with your left foot first, next to the dog's head, which cues him that you are moving forward.

loop on the chain part of the collar. Be sure to attach a *second choke collar and leash that you hold separately* because prong collars can come off during use, and you don't want to risk losing your dog. Do not use his identification collar for this, as non-choke collars can slip off if the dog pulls backward.

Hold the leash attached to the prong collar in your right hand, as described earlier, and slip your left hand through the loop of the extra "safety" leash, which remains inactive unless the prong collar falls off.

Repeat the exercise exactly as before. However, you will see a marked difference in the behavior of even a stubborn dog. The prongs are sharp enough to give quite a tweak, and no dog I have ever met will ignore it. Start off gently; use as *little force as necessary to get a response.*

Try to use the prong collar every other day at most, as constant use can make the dog's neck sore. As soon as you notice an improvement—the dog does not pull on the leash—return to using the ordinary chain choke collar. Use the prong collar only if the dog "forgets"; then go back to the regular collar as soon as you can afterward.

Note: Use the prong collar gently. It is engineered to be more severe than a regular choker. *Never use a prong collar in longeing* as it could damage the dog's hyoid bone in the neck.

HOUSEBREAKING

There are two ways to housebreak your dog. You can train him to relieve himself on newspapers on the floor ("paper training"), or you can teach him from the start to go outside whenever he needs to relieve himself.

It is simpler for the dog if you can teach him to go outside from the very start. For some people this may not be practical, so here are both methods.

Be sure to see "Urination Problems: Medical," in case the problem is a physical, not a training, problem.

DIRECT METHOD OF HOUSEBREAKING

Put your dog or puppy in a crate. (See "Crates.") Feed him there, and take him out after he eats, a half hour later, an hour later, and every hour throughout the day if possible. The aim is to *make it all but impossible for the dog to fail to do what you want him to do*—that is, to urinate and defecate out of doors rather than in his crate. The more frequently he succeeds (does his business where you want him to), the more often you can praise him with hugs, pats, and verbal praise. This makes it clear to him that he is behaving admirably and winning your approval each time he goes outside and does what he is supposed to do.

If he makes a mistake and makes a mess in his crate, show your disapproval briefly—only for a few seconds (say in a disgusted voice, "Oh, *no,* what a *disgusting* thing to do!") and *immediately* take the dog outside. As soon as he is outside, praise him as if nothing had ever gone wrong. You are trying to reinforce to him that when he is outside, all is well, and he can relax and do what he is supposed to. It is very important that no matter how disgusted you may actually feel by his mistake, you do not let him sense this once you are outside. Otherwise, you will make him think that there is no place that is all right to relieve himself in, because you show disapproval wherever he is.

It sometimes helps to return over and over to a spot outside where your dog or puppy has already relieved himself; he will smell the residue of past performances and be encouraged to use the same spot again.

Try tying a small bell (the "jingle bell" variety works best) to your doorknob. When you take your dog out, show him how to jingle the bell with his nose as you are about to open the door. By this method many dogs learn to let you know when they want to go out.

PAPER TRAINING

If it is impossible to get outside quickly or frequently enough (for instance, if you live on a high floor of an apartment building), paper train your dog first, then gradually transfer his location to the outdoors, as follows.

Confine your dog to a room with a bare floor that is easy to clean, such as a kitchen floor. Place newspapers over the entire surface. As soon as he leaves a mess, pick up and remove the soiled papers, and replace them with clean ones.

After a few days of this, leave half the floor covered with papers, the other half bare. If he soils the bare side, say with disgust in your voice, "Oh, *no,* what a *disgusting* thing to do!" and place him at once on the papers. Clean up the mess right away, using Nature's Miracle. (See "Odors.") When he learns to use the paper all the time, gradually over a period of a week or two reduce the size of the paper area on the floor until it is just big enough for him to use. Then begin phase two: Remove all papers from the floor.

Watch your dog like a hawk. If he shows signs of wanting to relieve himself (pacing, sniffing the floor, whining), immediately take him outside. Carry with you a few sheets of newspaper, which you will place on the ground outside. If he does not go immediately, be patient. Just stand quietly beside the papers, and try not to embarrass your dog by paying too much attention to him. Some dogs "freeze" and become too nervous to do their business.

When he makes any effort, praise him and take him for a walk before taking him back inside. Return to the paper each time you take him outside, as the smell will encourage him to use it again.

At the outset housebreaking a dog seems an impossible, daunting task. It seems that the dog will *never* learn. You may get discouraged and annoyed. Don't. *All* dogs learn housebreaking with consistent training as described. Yours will too. Just train *yourself* to realize that you will have to work through some errors of judgment on the dog's part before he learns how to modify his very natural behavior, and this takes a bit of time. You may have two or three weeks of intensive training before your dog really understands completely what is expected.

In thirty-five years of dog training, I have never met a dog who couldn't and didn't become perfectly housebroken, including some who had spent many years untrained. (They had lived outside in dog houses.) Housebreaking, except in rare cases where the problem is medical, *always* works, so just get on with the training, and keep calm.

HOUSEHOLD ITEMS THAT CAN HARM YOUR DOG

Some common items found in many households can harm or even kill your dog. Keep these items where a curious dog cannot get at them.

ANTIFREEZE

Antifreeze is deadly if your dog eats it. He will go into convulsions and die within minutes. Antifreeze tastes sweet, and dogs like to lick it. Watch to see if any spills on the garage floor, or drips from a leak.

STRING

Some dogs will chew any string. Almost any dog will chew and swallow string that has been used in cooking a chicken or turkey (to hold the feet together). After cooking, chop the string into short pieces and put it in the garbage. Keep the garbage where the dog can't get at it or open the garbage can. String eaten by a dog can wind around the intestine and kill him; it is often too late to save him by abdominal surgery when you discover the problem has occurred. Prevention is the cure.

PANTYHOSE

For reasons known best to themselves, some dogs will eat pantyhose and stockings. Like string, these can kill your dog. Don't leave pantyhose or stockings drying in places your dog has access to.

PILLS

Just like small children, dogs must never have access to medicines of any kind. Keep them in a cupboard high up, in safety-closed containers.

CHICKEN OR PORK BONES

These splinter and can puncture your dog's intestines. Veal bones can also splinter, as do turkey bones or duck bones. The *only* bones you can safely give your dog to chew on are large beef shin bones (the part in the middle, not the knuckle ends, which can cause impaction as the dog can chew up large quantities of bone and swallow it). Some people say proudly that they have fed their dog all sorts of bones all his life without ill effects; for every such tale, there are many cases of dogs who died of a punctured intestine from eating the wrong sort of bone.

POISONS

Puppies and young dogs will try eating almost anything. Keep weed killer, flea spray, drain cleaners, insect repellent, ant traps, and anything else that you wouldn't eat yourself out of the reach of your dog. Even an adult dog, with time on his paws, may decide to chew up an interesting-looking box. Keep all such items safely locked in a cabinet where the dog cannot reach them.

POP-OUT PLASTIC "DONENESS" INDICATORS FROM CHICKEN OR TURKEY

These are particularly dangerous, because they smell and taste good to a dog but can be deadly if eaten. Treat these devices like dangerous bones, placing them where your dog cannot get at them (in a plastic bag in the refrigerator on a high shelf, for instance).

CHEMICAL LAWN SPRAYS

No fewer than eight different people have told me within the past ten months that their dogs have died, or been destroyed by their veterinarians, after having walked or played on lawns treated with chemicals. While no one can prove beyond legal doubt yet that these chemicals are deadly to dogs (and perhaps also to children), there is little doubt in the minds of these former dog owners that lawn treatment chemicals caused their pets' deaths. All these dogs died from lymphoma, a virulent systemic cancer. I am prohibited by law from naming specific lawn-treatment systems and lawn-care products to avoid, but my advice as a dog trainer is not to use any chemicals on grass where dogs will walk or play and to avoid walking on grass that indicates, usually with small flags posted nearby, that it has been treated with chemicals. One dog who ate grass from a treated lawn died of cancer that ran the length of her throat.

IDENTIFICATION TAGS AND TATTOOING

Identification tags should remain on your dog's permanent collar (the one you don't remove except when your dog is in his crate, not on the choker collar) at all times. No one expects his dog to get lost, slip out the back door, and go calling on another dog in the neighborhood or next town. But these things can happen. Your best line of defense is an ID tag. You can buy identification tags, unengraved, at pet stores or vets' offices.

The best ones are made of stainless steel, engraved by the

company you buy them from. (You usually have to mail the tags away, and they are sent back a few days later, engraved.) They are customarily engraved on only one side, but for an extra dollar you can get information engraved on both sides. This is worth doing, because even stainless steel can be difficult to read if several tags rub against each other over a period of time. (To minimize the abrasive effect, see "Identification Tags: Preventing Them from Jingling.")

Other tags made of a plastic or composition material in bright colors, such as red or yellow, are available; they have the advantage of being easy to read. Check the tags periodically to be sure that the lettering remains legible and that the tags have not broken or chipped.

On the form you fill out and mail in to the company for engraving, there is a place for your name, the name of the dog, your address, and so on. I recommend that you ignore all this and print the following words on the form:

Large Reward For Return
(xxx) xxx-xxxx
(xxx) xxx-xxxx
(xxx) xxx-xxxx

The x's represent your *home telephone number* (with area code), your *work number,* and the *telephone number of your vet* or a very reliable friend or relative.

Most people who find a lost dog will return him without accepting a reward. For someone who would not otherwise take the time and trouble to return your dog or even to give you a call, the money incentive may well make the difference between getting your dog back and his death by being hit by a car, being killed in a so-called animal shelter, or dying in any of a number of other ways. With such people I have found that $25 is considered large enough for the dog to be returned.

Identification Tags

Have ID tags engraved on one side with the words "Large Reward for Return," and on the other list your home and work telephone numbers, and the number of your veterinarian.

TATTOOING YOUR DOG: ANOTHER METHOD OF IDENTIFICATION

The National Dog Registry, an organization in operation for nearly twenty-five years, is dedicated to the task of reuniting lost or stolen pets with their owners.

A major source of concern to this organization is the fact that many of these dogs and cats end up in research laboratories. The Registry cites heartbreaking case histories. Yet many research laboratories now feel public pressure to look for tattooed numbers on dogs and cats that they purchase for experimentation and to return these animals to their owners. The National Dog Registry has worked long and hard to force research facilities to understand that tattooed pets *must* be returned to their owners; its work includes seminars for research lab personnel to learn how the public feels about the issues.

A veterinarian can tattoo a dog permanently, quickly, and nearly painlessly. The usual location is on the inside of the dog's upper hind leg. Hair needs to be kept clipped away from the tattoo so it remains visible. Important: Tattooed pets can be traced to their owners only if the tattoo is registered.

For more information write to the National Dog Registry, Box 116, Woodstock, New York 12498.

IDENTIFICATION TAGS: PREVENTING THEM FROM JINGLING

The noise from dog identification tags banging against a rabies tag and municipal license tag can be quite annoying. Imagine how it sounds to your dog, with his ears so close to the source of the noise and his acute sense of hearing.

The solution is simple: Take a rubber band and wrap it around all the tags so they will not jingle. You will have to replace the rubber band periodically when it wears out or breaks.

ILLNESS: WARNING SIGNS

Many illnesses can be cured if attended to promptly. Signs that your dog may need medical attention include the following.

Anal rubbing and irritation
Bad breath
Bizarre behavior (walking in circles endlessly, standing and staring at a wall, sudden unprovoked aggression, failure to stand up, etc.)
Blood in urine or stool
Bluish gums or tongue
Broken bones
Constipation
Coughing
Cuts and abrasions of severe nature

Preventing Identification Tags from Jingling
Use a rubber band to hold identification tags, rabies vaccination tags, and municipal dog license tags together so they won't jingle.

Drooling (in absence of food)
Excessive gas (flatulence)
Excessive water drinking
Extreme itchiness of skin
Fainting or dizziness
Fever
Gagging
Hair loss
Huge appetite without weight gain
Hunched posture, back curved upward in middle
Inability to defecate
Increased urination
Irregular or very fast heartbeat
Jaundice
Labored breathing
Lack of coordination (sudden onset)
Limping or dragging a leg
Loss of appetite
Mucus with stool
Off-color stools (either white or black and tarry)
Oversensitivity to light
Pus in urine
Runny nose
Scratching constantly at ears or eyes
Seizures
Shivering (in absence of cold ambient temperature)
Straining to urinate
Swelling in any part of the body, especially around eyes
Swollen legs
Swollen stomach
Tilting of head or shaking head repeatedly
Vomiting, especially if repeated more than once in a short
   time
Watery or gummy eyes
Wax in ears in abnormal amounts, especially with foul odor

Weight loss
Whitish film over or in eye

Here are the vital signs of a normal, healthy dog at rest.

Temperature: 100 to 102.5°F
Pulse: 70 beats per minute
Respiration: 20 breaths per minute
Gum "Refill Time" (the time it takes for the gums, when pressed with your finger, to return to healthy pink color from white color where you pressed the gum): 2 seconds
Skin Turger: Skin lifted upward from the scruff of dog's neck should immediately fall back into place when released. Failure to do so can indicate dehydration.

INTRODUCING TWO DOGS FOR THE FIRST TIME

If you already have one dog and want to bring another into your home on a permanent basis, it is important to remember that the first dog will feel that the newcomer is invading his territory. In order to minimize his feelings of being invaded, make the introduction gradual and, if possible, over a period of at least a few days.

If it is feasible, have the new dog merely visit your home for a half hour or so the first time. Show your own dog by your attitude toward him that he is still number-one dog in your affections and that you do not intend to replace him with the new dog. Do this by placing an arm around him while he sits close by you, on a leash, with another person holding the new dog a few feet away on another leash. If there is any chance that a fight might occur, do not let the dogs closer to one another than four or five feet the first time they meet.

Take both dogs, separated by four or five feet at all times, for a walk together. This is one of the most effective ways of getting two dogs who might feel adversarial toward each other to accept one another. Walking them far enough so they get physically tired will work in your favor. If both are males, they will mark (urinate) frequently on trees, posts, and bushes; let them take their time sniffing and give each a chance to mark *over* the spot where the other has urinated. This gives each dog the feeling that he has made himself known to the neighborhood as being at least on a par with, if not superior to, the other dog. Male dogs also will scratch the earth after they mark with urine; this leaves a trace of scent from the soles of their feet (the only part of a dog that readily sweats) and likewise serves to show that they are big and strong and vigorous. Give both dogs plenty of time to go through these posturings; they matter deeply to male dogs.

Females also will mark by urinating but in general are less interested in this territorial claiming exercise than males.

On the second visit, again walk the dogs together, and be alert for a time when they both appear friendly and interested in getting to know each other better. With two males, be careful; if there is any sign of aggression, follow instructions for "Aggression with Other Dogs."

If it is evident from the start that both dogs will not fight, then these guidelines may not be necessary. But the first dog always will feel threatened to some degree by arrival of a newcomer, even a new puppy. It is therefore highly important that you *always* treat the first dog as dog number one: that is, feed him first, pat him first, and if he interrupts your patting of the second dog with a nudge or other demand for attention, stop patting Number Two and pat Number One for a moment, showing him that he has retained his primary spot in the hierarchy of your "pack."

If two dogs show signs of ill will (growling, stiff-legged walking, general unfriendliness), place them in crates side by side, separated by four or five inches (so no one's tail will be chewed up by the other dog if it accidentally pokes into the wrong crate). If either dog growls while in his crate, yell "Hey!" and bang hard on the top of the crate with a book or shoe.

Both dogs will take their cue from your own behavior. Show clearly and immediately that you do not like and will not tolerate shows of aggression and that you approve of shows of friendliness.

Note: Are Two Dogs Easier Than One? Almost always! Two dogs give each other constant companionship, which most dogs like because their instinct is to be part of a pack. It is pleasant and reassuring for them to sleep leaning against each other, to chew on each other's ears, to play bitey games and romp in ways that you may not want to do as often as your dog does. It gives you a breather from "being a dog" twenty-four hours a day. (Don't forget, you are pack leader to your dog.) Your *two* dogs can keep each other company when you are at work and teach each other things. (Dogs learn from watching another dog being taught to sit or stay, for instance.) Dogs develop better appetites where there is another dog for competition at meal time, and quickly learn to eat raw carrots and broccoli and cabbage (all possible cancer preventers) when they know that if they turn up their nose at the vegetable, the other dog will grab it.

If you have two dogs, be sure you never leave them alone while wearing choker collars. The reason is important: When playing, one dog may hook his bottom canine teeth under the collar of his friend, and lie down and roll on his back, thus strangling the other dog. If you ever do see this happen, simply take the dog who is lying down by the *hind legs* and turn him over so the other dog's collar is released. While playing alone, make sure both dogs wear only collars that are made of rolled leather or nylon webbing, fitted snugly enough so there is barely room for two fingers between the collar and the dog's neck.

Before I knew to take off choker collars on unattended dogs, I saw two of my own dogs playing in just this way and was shocked to see how easily one nearly choked the other. If I hadn't happened to be there, the choked dog would have died.

ITCHY SKIN ("HOT SPOTS")

Intensely itchy skin sometimes called "hot spots," can make a dog's life miserable. Itchy skin can be caused by fleas, allergies to food, airborne dust mites or pollen, too-low a level of testosterone, among many other causes. You may have an idea of the cause yourself; or it may take your vet to help you find a solution.

A dog who is hypersensitive to fleas may go into violent fits of scratching and biting at his skin. Even one flea on a dog who is especially sensitive to fleas can cause an allergic reaction. (See "Fleas.")

But be cautious of a diagnosis calling for cortisone injections or pills. (And *ask* your veterinarian if a medication he prescribes is cortisone-based.) Cortisone almost magically relieves itching temporarily, but also causes deterioration of the body's vital organs, including kidneys and liver. And as soon as the cortisone stops, the itching begins again. Cortisone is not a cure, merely a temporary stop-gap. Look for the true cause instead, and do not subject your dog unnecessarily to a damaging drug.

One treatment without dangerous side effects is a combination of polyunsaturated essential fatty acids (Derm Caps is one brand name; they are dissolving capsules given twice daily) and antihistamines (a brand name for one kind is Atarex, given two or three times daily).

If the problem is underproduction of testosterone in male dogs, a veterinarian will prescribe testosterone in tablet form.

Acupuncture can help certain skin conditions and should be considered. (See "Acupuncture.")

In many cases bathing a dog at least once a month may help, especially if the problem is fleas. But too-frequent bathing can dry your dog's skin and itself cause itching. Be sure to use only a shampoo especially formulated for dogs, an extra-conditioning shampoo (Pert is one good brand), or baby shampoo; the harsher shampoos can cause allergic reactions.

If your dog scratches to the point where there are actually open red patches on his skin, see your veterinarian; secondary infection can set in.

If the cause is dry skin (which many older dogs have), rubbing Vaseline into the itchy area often relieves the problem immediately. This may be an area where there is normally little or no hair, such as on the inside of the hind legs or belly, or it may be somewhere the dog has rubbed off the hair due to itching skin, such as the underside of the chin. Rub plenty of Vaseline into the area three or four times a day; it will alleviate the itching at once. Even in areas with heavy fur, such as the back of the dog near the tail (a frequent site of "hot spots") Vaseline rubbed in may help substantially.

JEALOUSY OF ANOTHER PET OR PERSON

Dogs are very much like people in that they usually choose the person they think nicest, most "cool," or most admirable, and seek to make a special bond with that person.

A dog may then resent another pet, child, or adult human being's getting near his chosen object of affections. While this is perfectly normal behavior, it is not acceptable for the dog to show his affection in this way.

If possible, the person whom the dog loves best should discipline the dog. For instance, if a dog likes a wife best, and her husband finds the dog tries to get physically between him and his wife, the wife should follow the instructions given for "Aggression with People." If the person the dog likes best is not able to discipline the dog, someone else can do it, but the person being "protected" by the dog should use his voice to make it clear that he also does not appreciate having the dog show his affection in this way. As the dog gets between a wife and her husband, for instance, the wife should say to the dog "No!" or "Hey!" and a second person can administer the physical correction (a jumping bat or book, as described on pages 138 and 23) at the same moment. It is extremely important that the dog meet a united front of disapproval. Corrections will not work if the dog believes the object of his affections secretly wants him to "protect" her or him.

Sometimes a dog will become jealous of a new baby or small child. If the dog shows any signs of being overly curious or aggressive toward a baby or child, do not allow them to be together without having the dog under control on a leash. When the dog pulls toward the child, make him sit instead. Use a sharp, quick jerk on the leash attached to his choke collar if necessary. Let him look at the baby or child without coming closer than six or eight feet until he shows only mild interest.

A dog jealous of another pet will seek to prevent the other

pet from being near the person he likes best. In this case, the person should correct the dog with a jumping bat (see below) using methods described in "Aggression."

Any sign of aggressive or overly possessive behavior must be corrected, or it can lead to biting. If you are not getting good results yourself in correcting it, call in a professional trainer without delay.

See also "Sulking."

All these problems are helped markedly by obedience training. Teach your dog to heel, sit, stay, down, and come when called, as outlined under various headings in this book (see Contents) for page numbers.

JUMPING BAT

A jumping bat, similar to a riding crop for horses but sturdier, is a tool you will need to make corrections to your dog's behavior.

A jumping bat is about fifteen inches to eighteen inches long, with a triangular tab at the end about an inch across. You can buy a bat at a riding goods store for about $10 or less. Some are made entirely of rubber with a fiberglass center for stiffness; others are covered with leather or cloth.

Hit the palm of your own hand with the tab end of the bat, and you will see that while it stings, it does not really hurt you. Use the bat when you know that your dog *knows* he has done something he is not permitted to do. For instance, if you have forbidden his getting up on furniture, and you then find him curled comfortably on the couch when he thought you had gone out, you would use the bat to emphasize that he must not do this.

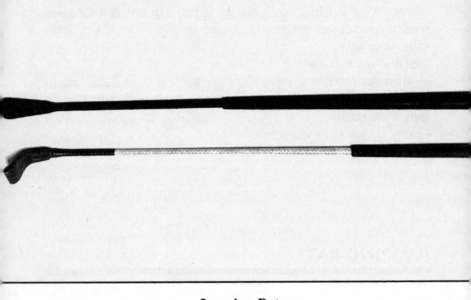

Jumping Bat
A tool to reinforce your corrections of your dog's behavior

Use the bat in this way: *Put a leash on the dog first,* if you believe there is any chance that he may try to bite your hand when you correct him with the bat. Hold the front end of the dog up by the leash, so that his front feet are off the floor by a few inches. This will make it more difficult for him to move around when you swat him with the bat. Give him a swat with the tab end of the bat hard enough to sting, but not hard enough to harm him. You will know how hard to swat because you've already tried it out on your own hand. The *only* place to swat a dog with a bat is on his thigh—the upper part of his hind leg, where the leg is "meaty." Do not swat anywhere near his head, as you could injure his eyes.

As you swat him sharply once or twice, say "Hey!" loudly. This teaches him to associate the word with an unpleasant action; in time, the word alone will be enough to make him cease behavior you don't want him to do.

Immediately after swatting the dog's back thigh with a moderate but stinging tap, hit the floor with the bat using *all* your force. It should make a good loud noise and will make your dog say to himself, "Uh-oh, that bat can really be scary. I'm lucky I only got a tap with it, since I see how terrible it can really be." Hit the floor three or four times as hard as you can in rapid succession, and say loudly "Hey!" each time. Keep the dog on a short leash nearby with your free hand. Be very careful you do not accidentally strike the dog; he will probably pull back away from you as much as he can.

Then unsnap the leash and ignore your dog for a few minutes as if nothing had happened. Let him go off and think about the lesson for a while before you "change the subject" by offering a walk or a new command.

If the dog shows any sign of aggression, however, see "Aggression."

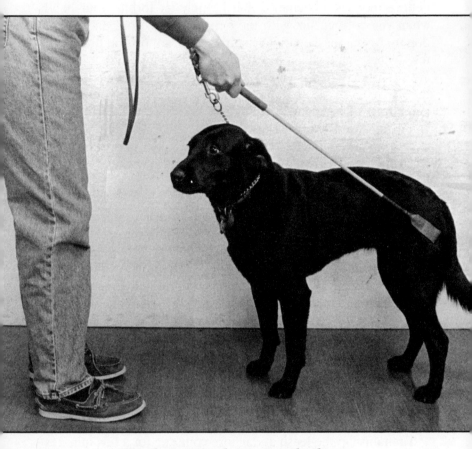

*Use the jumping bat to swat the dog on
the upper hind thigh, where the leg is "meaty."*

JUMPING UP ON PEOPLE

Dogs often want to jump up on people they like, especially when they are excited. Usually they will show this behavior when they greet you after not having seen you for a while, or when you offer a walk or food. Although it is quite normal for a dog to want to show affection or excitement by jumping up on you, it is annoying and should not be allowed.

Be sure that you are absolutely consistent about refusing to allow your dog to jump up on you. Some people allow it "just this once." By making even one exception, you confuse the dog and mess up the training. The rule is, don't let your dog jump up on any person for any reason at any time.

To break a dog of the habit of jumping up on you, be ready so that when he jumps up, you can act instantly and without hesitation. The swiftness with which you correct him is half the battle. The moment the dog's front feet leave the floor is the time to act.

Do two things at the same instant. Raise your knee *fast* and jab it into the dog's chest or stomach. (This sounds hard on the dog, but it won't hurt him. It will just be extremely uncomfortable for the moment that he is jumping up, which is necessary to train him.) At the same time, say "No!" or "Hey!" or "Out!" (This last is said to sound like a dog's bark. Any word will do, but always use the same word.)

If the dog is very small, such as a toy poodle or small terrier, of course you cannot use your knee. In this case, have the flat of your hand come down squarely on top of the dog's head, making a smacking sound like a slap. Again, this will not hurt the dog, but it will correct him by making it unpleasant for the moment he is jumping up, which is essential to training him.

Sometimes very large dogs can ignore a knee jab, and you may be more successful by stepping with your toe on their hind toes. Be sure not to do this too hard, as dogs' feet are delicate and you could break a bone. Sometimes you can simply push the dog's hind feet sideways with your own foot when he is jumping up on you. This will cause him to lose his balance. In any case, whichever method you use, also use a verbal command, such as "Hey!" at the same time. This is necessary to teach the dog to respect the command alone, so that eventually you will need only to say the word to have the dog respond correctly (and not jump up on you).

If the dog jumps up on other people who are unable to correct him, such as small children or very elderly people, or merely people who don't like or understand dogs, it is your job to correct him. As before, being ready for the event is important. Position yourself near the other person if you suspect your dog may jump up. Use your own knee or hand to correct the dog. If it is impossible to position yourself to do this, use a large, thin, flat book (children's books are good) and smack the dog on the top of his head with the flat of the book. Use the command word you have chosen at the same time.

It may help to place your dog in sit position (have his choker collar and leash on him) before guests are expected. If your dog stops jumping up on you but continues to jump up on other people, you should keep him away from other people while you give him a sterner correction. Have an assistant help you. Get the dog into a situation where he is likely to jump up on the assistant (such as letting the assistant walk in carrying a leash or a dog biscuit). When the dog jumps up, *bellow* the correction word at him in a truly frightening, huge voice. Try to scare him by making it *loud.* At the same time, give the dog a much more severe physical correction. The moment his feet return to the floor, give him one fast swat with your hand on top of his head for good measure. Jerk down once or twice on his collar. Then repeat the exercise, having the assistant walk into the room with leash or dog biscuit. If you have done the work right, the dog will not jump up this time. Praise him, bend down and give him a few hugs, but be ready for him, in his exuberance at being praised, to jump up again. If he does, correct him swiftly and severely.

It is easy to tell when you are correcting a dog "enough." If so, he will cease the undesirable behavior. If he continues more than two or three times despite your corrections, you have not been fast enough in giving the correction or else not administered the deterrent with sufficient severity to discourage the behavior.

KENNEL COUGH

If your dog suddenly develops a dry, hacking cough, especially if he has been in company with other dogs (such as after a visit to a boarding kennel), he may have kennel cough. Kennel cough, which is caused by a number of viruses, is passed very quickly from one dog to another. If you have more than one dog, you will need to isolate the coughing dog in a warm room where the air is not too dry. (Boil a pan of water and leave it in the room, or place a pot of water on a radiator.) Your veterinarian will determine if kennel cough is the problem and, if so, prescribe antibiotics to prevent complications. Although kennel cough is not much more serious than a bad cold in a human being, if left untreated, it can lead to life-threatening complications such as pneumonia.

If your dog coughs, sneezes frequently, has labored breathing, or otherwise seems to be breathing in a way different from his normal pattern, a veterinarian should check him at once.

Prior to leaving your dog in a boarding kennel, have your veterinarian administer the temporary kennel cough preventive by nasal spray. Many kennels now require proof of this protection prior to admitting a dog.

LOST DOG:
HOW TO FIND YOUR PET IF HE GETS LOST

By far the best solution is prevention. See "Identification Tags and Tattooing." Make sure your dog cannot get over or under any fence you confine him in. Never leave a dog unattended, even in a yard or on a cable. Never leave a dog tied up outside a store or anywhere else during your walks. Treat your dog much as you would a two- or three-year-old child, and you won't be far wrong. Dognapping is unfortunately very prevalent today. (See "Dognapping.")

If your dog does get lost, do the following immediately:

- Call the local police station. Give a full description of your dog, including color, size, weight, markings, length of fur, whether ears stand up (like a shepherd) or hang down (like a retriever).
- Call the local animal shelter(s) and give the same description.
- Drive, walk, or ride a bike around your neighborhood, calling your dog. Take along food he likes, especially if it has a good strong smell, like cat food.
- Call all veterinarians in your area, including those in neighboring towns. Post a flyer with photograph of your dog on vets' notice boards. Call them daily.
- Put up posters everywhere in and near your town. Offer a reward. Describe the dog fully. Use a photograph as well if possible. You can photocopy it in color on standard $8\frac{1}{2} \times 11$-inch paper.
- Go *daily* to the local animal shelters and look for your dog. Shelters are not especially good at reuniting dogs with their families. I know of many, many cases where frantic owners looked for their pets in shelters and found them there, even though they had asked on the telephone previ-

ously and had been told no dog fitting that description was impounded. *Go in person every day.*

- Call the police station daily. They will not hold the dog themselves, and most don't care particularly about stray dogs' finding their owners. But if they hear from you daily, your chances are better that they will remember you and your dog.

Note that crackpots may answer your posters, with unpleasant messages. If such a person calls you up, be polite and matter-of-fact. Do not get emotional (that is what they mostly want). State firmly that you are offering a substantial cash reward for the safe return of your dog. Then say thank you, and hang up. If the person calls back, repeat yourself, over and over as needed. Do not vary the message. He or she will get tired of harassing you after a while.

You also may want to place an ad in your local newspaper, on the most popular supermarket bulletin boards, on school bulletin boards, and anywhere else where people are likely to see it. The key to finding your lost dog is persistence. Don't give up, and do follow up daily.

MANGE

Mange is actually a general designation given to several kinds of mites. Mites can live in the dog's ears, beneath the skin, or on any other part of the body.

A dog with *ear mites* will have intense itching in his ears. He may scratch around and in his ears with his hind foot, shake his head repeatedly, or try to scrape his head against furniture or the floor. If you rub gently inside his ear with a tissue or cotton swab, you will find a lot of wax, dark colored and smelly. You will need to have the dog examined by a veterinarian, who will prescribe special insect-killing topical treatments to use at home until the problem is eliminated.

Scabies is a form of mange caused by mites that burrow underneath the dog's skin, causing violent itching and loss of hair. If untreated, eventually the dog can lose all his hair. A vet will examine a scraping of your dog's skin under a microscope and prescribe topical insecticides and antibiotics to fight the secondary infection that can occur from scratching. Both other dogs and human beings can get scabies from an infected dog.

Demodectic mange causes red, lumpy patches of skin and itching. A vet diagnoses the condition by taking a skin scraping, as for scabies.

MARKING

When you walk your dog, be sure to allow him time to walk while *not* in heel position. Every dog needs to mark territory in order to communicate normally with other dogs in the neighborhood. Preventing this behavior would be something like allowing a person to walk around the neighborhood, but blindfolding his eyes and tying his hands to his side, and not allowing him to speak to anyone he might meet. Dogs leave messages for other dogs and "read" the messages left by other dogs. To prevent this is at best unkind to your dog and will make him anxious and unhappy.

When your dog has sniffed around a tree during his walk, he will usually lift his leg (males) or scooch down (females) and urinate. Your dog is leaving a marker for other dogs who will pass by. He is claiming this territory as his, or leaving a message for a particular dog. If you have a male and a female, the female will usually mark first, and the male will mark over or near where she marked. This says to other dogs "Paws off my lady friend, she's with *me.*"

Many dogs—nearly all males, neutered or not, and even some females—will scratch the dirt with their hind legs after they urinate. Some will even use their front legs at the same time, backing up in order to leave a longer track.

This curious behavior makes perfect sense from a dog's point of view. The dog's pads sweat, leaving a strong scent for the next dog who comes along to take note of. By scraping the earth, a dog says to whoever comes by next: "I am a big, tough dog, someone to be noticed and reckoned with. Here is my scent [urine] and here, next to that is the size of my footprints." By making vigorous scratches in the earth, your dog shows his vitality and, presumably, his size.

However, dogs are not above contriving to fool other dogs. Even a tiny dog can scratch the ground, moving backward, for a long distance. You may see a pug or Pekingese leave a track six feet long. ("My, what a *huge* dog left this mark!" the next dog will think.)

Let your dog leave his mark; knowing that he will be taken note of is reassuring to a dog.

MATTED FUR

Long-haired dogs and dogs with fuzzy fur are prone to hair matting, especially just behind their ears, on the backs of their legs where hair may grow especially long, and on other parts of their bodies.

The best way to prevent hairballs and matting from forming on your dog is to brush him daily. It is relatively easy to disentangle hair that is beginning to mat up before it gets really tangled. Even burrs, which are easy to pick up if you walk through a field in the fall, can be pulled out with little difficulty if you act promptly.

If a dog has matted fur that is impossible to disentangle, use a pair of nail scissors and very carefully snip the hair, holding it in place until you can remove the matting. Be careful that the dog does not move suddenly and cause you to stab him accidentally. Use an assistant if necessary.

You will have to put up with a patch or two of cut-off fur for a while until it grows back in.

MEETING A DOG YOU DO NOT KNOW:
THE BEST WAY TO INTRODUCE YOURSELF

There is an old theory that when you meet a dog you do not know, you should stick out your hand, palm down, and let him sniff the back of your hand.

This is, in fact, a bad practice. By sticking your hand toward a dog who does not know you, and who may be very wary or even frightened, you threaten him by invading his space. He cannot be sure, when your hand comes toward him, that you do not intend to grab him.

A much better practice is to stand normally, let your hand lie against your own thigh, and then tap your fingers against your leg, making your hand behave rather like a dog's tail wagging. As you do this, speak reassuringly to the dog. *Let him come to you* rather than you going to him. If you continue to "wag your tail," most dogs will recognize the gesture as a sign of friendliness, and some even will wag their own tails in response.

Make no attempt to go to the dog until he has shown desire to meet you first.

Do not stoop down or sit to be "at his level." This creates a challenging situation to a dog.

Do not stare into his eyes, for the same reason. Look down and to the side.

MUZZLES

A muzzle holds a dog's jaws shut. A dog wearing a properly adjusted muzzle cannot bite you. In certain circumstances—with an injured, badly frightened, or traumatized dog, or during procedures like nail-clipping—a muzzle can make life much easier for you.

Keep the muzzle on the dog for the shortest possible time in order to achieve what you must. For instance, put a muzzle on your dog *after* you arrive at the veterinarian's office (while still on familiar turf inside your own car, where the dog is less stressed) rather than making him wear it on the drive to the vet's.

A Muzzle
A properly adjusted leather strap muzzle

Also remember that in hot weather, or when a dog is extremely upset, he must be able to pant or he will overheat and can become seriously ill. Be aware of this especially during hot months of the year.

There are four types of muzzle; all work comparably well.

- A *Velcro* muzzle consists of two straps of nylon webbing with Velcro on one side. Adjust the nose loop to fit snugly around your dog's muzzle and the other strap to fit snugly behind his ears.
- A leather strap muzzle fits a sort of basket of straps to encase the dog's muzzle, with a strap fitting behind the ears. They come in sizes marked by number; you will need to try the muzzle on your dog to be sure it is the right size.
- A wire-screen mesh muzzle places a basket of screen, something like window screen only stronger, around the dog's nose, held in place by a leather strap behind the dog's ears. With this type of muzzle, the dog can open his mouth somewhat inside the wire cage, although he still cannot pant normally.
- A homemade version can be made from a pair of pantyhose or a strip of cotton flannel ($2\frac{1}{2}$ feet long by 2 inches wide for a medium-size dog). Tie a loose single knot in the middle of the strip of cloth, leaving the knot hole big enough to fit easily around your dog's muzzle. Slip the hole over your dog's nose, with the knot underneath (next to his lower jaw, near his chin). Bring the ends of the cloth back and pull the knot firmly tight as you do so, closing the dog's jaws snugly. Tie the loose ends of the cloth behind the dog's ears in a bow. When you are ready to remove the muzzle, pull one end of the bow.

Use care putting on and removing a muzzle; some severely stressed dogs will try to bite you. Move slowly, talk to the dog as you proceed, and try to make the process as unobtrusive as possible throughout. Make no sudden moves. It pays to get the dog used to the muzzle before you really need to use it.

NAILS: CLIPPING

Your veterinarian or a grooming parlor can clip your dog's nails for you, but doing it yourself is not difficult, and much less expensive.

Buy a very good nail cutter at a pet supply store. Avoid the little flimsy ones, and find a pair of clippers that feels good and substantial. It will cost between $10 and $15, but will last many times as long as the cheaper ones and will cut more effectively from the start.

Also buy a muzzle. (See "Muzzles.") Soft ones consisting of two bands of nylon webbing, one to fit around the dog's head behind his ears, the other around his muzzle, each band held in place by an adjustable piece of Velcro, can be bought at most veterinarians'. Leather muzzles are more expensive.

Put the muzzle on your dog with as little fuss as possible. Take him to a well-lighted area, either a large table or on the floor if you can work comfortably there. Look closely at his nails in a bright light. Each nail has an area of "old" nail and an area of highly sensitive living nail, exactly like your own nails and quick.

By careful observation, you will be able to see where the quick ends and the old, insensitive nail begins. Cut only the old nail. Be sure to cut the pointed end off the dew claw (the dog's "thumb"). If in doubt, err on the side of leaving too much nail, rather than cutting too close to the quick. You always can go back a day later and trim further. But if you accidentally cut the dog's quick, he will yelp, may try to bite you to make you stop hurting him (the muzzle will prevent this), and will begin to find having his nails cut a traumatic experience.

If, despite your best efforts, you do accidentally cut the dog's quick, speak soothingly to him and move to another foot entirely before trying again. On this foot, cut the merest sliver off one or two nails. Now your aim is to minimize your dog's fear about the process, to make him see that nothing painful usually happens, and then to quit and leave it for another day.

There is nothing to be gained from hurting or traumatizing your dog. Take your time, spread the procedure out over two or three days if necessary, and teach your dog that there is nothing to fear. Eventually you will be able to dispense with the muzzle.

If a nail bleeds, the dog will lick it off until it stops bleeding. You can stop the bleeding with a styptic pencil (the same as used in stopping razor nicks) or powder, but the dog will lick it off unless you prevent him, so it is easier to let him just lick the cut himself.

ODORS: REMOVING FOUL SMELLS

Dogs like to roll in things that smell, apparently to them, quite interesting, but that offend the human nose.

If your dog rolls in something foul-smelling, your only recourse is to wash the dog. (See "Baths.")

If the foul odor is something your dog, or possibly you yourself, tracked into the house, use soap and water, then Nature's Miracle, a liquid stain and odor remover available at pet stores and veterinary clinics, which dismantles the smell at the chemical level. It has almost no scent of its own, works on the enzyme principle, and is highly effective in removing smells as if they were never there.

Remember to wash the cover of your dog's bed frequently— once a week at least. If the cover of your dog's bed can't be removed, make a washable cover out of an old dark-colored or patterned sheet or other cloth.

OLD AGE

An old dog who is happy and comfortable is a beautiful sight. It means that someone has done an excellent job of taking care of the dog and making his life worthwhile; it says very good things about the dog's human companion.

Old dogs suffer from the same sorts of inconveniences that old human beings do: Their joints get stiff, their energy level diminishes, their hearing lessens or ceases altogether, their eyesight becomes less acute. Luckily for dogs, their primary information system, the sense of smell, remains strong.

Dogs are realists, much more pragmatic and practical than most people. They live in the present and do not worry greatly about the past or, very much, the future. They focus on what is going on right now, this minute. If some of a dog's situation at present is good and some of it is bad, a dog will pay attention to the good part of his situation and ignore, insofar as possible, the bad. For instance, if your dog is confined to his crate, even for several hours such as while you are at work, he will generally just curl up and go to sleep to pass the time, rather than fret about the injustice of staying home while you go somewhere without him. In the same way, your dog adjusts to old age or even illness; he makes the best of it and enjoys all he can of life despite it.

Old dogs appreciate a soft, warm bed; their circulation is not as good as that of a younger dog. (See "Beds for Dogs.") Be sure there are no drafts where he sleeps. A bed with sides, or a thick, soft dog bed (good ones are available from the L.L. Bean catalog in Freeport, Maine, and various pet stores) are good choices. There are also "orthopedic" beds consisting of foam rubber shaped like the inside of an egg box, in little cones, said to be comfortable to older dogs. Do not use electric blankets or heating pads because, as for elderly people, they could burn your dog, and he may be insensitive to this in his old age. Also, a dog may dig around in his bed and short-circuit a wire, causing a fire.

Choose food for an elderly dog carefully. Cornucopia, Eukanuba, Science Diet, and other brands available at pet stores and supermarkets are designed for old dogs. Even better are certain formulas, both dry and canned, available only through veterinarians. These include KD Formula (for kidney disease) by Prescription Diet, specially formulated to ease stress on an aging dog's kidneys, and other specially designed formulas. Ask your vet for recommendations based on your dog's health.

Vitamin and mineral supplements can be of great help. A fifteen-year old dog of our family's still gallops and moves almost like a dog many years younger, although his energy is not as great as in the past. This is possibly due in good part to a comprehensive vitamin/mineral supplement regimen designed for him by a veterinarian; the difference in his alertness and activity is noticeable compared to a year ago before he began this regimen.

Give an old dog as much exercise as he will take, but do not overtax him. Go slowly if he wants to go slowly, give him plenty of time to sniff the bushes or lampposts, don't hurry him. Take an old dog out several times a day rather than on one long walk.

Incontinence is sometimes a problem for old dogs. The

causes are many. (See "Urination Problems: Medical.") Do not scold an old dog for something he cannot help. To make the problem of incontinence much easier to deal with, fold a towel lengthwise, place it around the waist of a male dog, and secure it with safety pins. Under the towel tuck a disposable baby diaper (one cut in half is just the right size) where the dog's urine comes out. It is possible to rig up a diaper for female dogs also, but you will have to secure it to the dog's collar or it will slip off backward. (See note on "piddle pants" under "Urination Problems: Medical.") Wash the dog off periodically to prevent diaper rash.

Another solution is to keep your dog on a washable surface, such as a kitchen floor, covered with a thick layer of newspapers. Remove the papers as they become wet.

Be sure an old dog has plenty of water at all times. Old dogs can become dehydrated more easily than younger ones. If your dog shows signs of dehydration, try adding extra water to his food, making meals a sort of soup of dog food. (The skin should, when pulled up from the dog's back, quickly return to its normal place when you let go of it. If it seems to stay pulled up for a second or two after you release it, the dog may be dehydrated. If the condition persists, see your vet.)

If you have other dogs or small children, see that they do not tire out the old dog by rough or continuous play. Give an old dog plenty of time to rest and snooze.

If your dog becomes deaf, as most dogs do somewhere between the ages of ten and twelve, teach him hand signals. Contrary to the saying, you *can* teach an old dog new tricks. Some dogs with impaired hearing can still hear a sharp loud hand-clap. Use this hand-clap to get his attention, then motion sharply with one hand toward your body. Gently pull the dog toward you until he understands what you want, then praise him with pats and hugs. This is one time when giving a food reward, such as a piece of cheese, may be a good idea.

Old dogs may become more forgetful than when they were young. Some literally forget to come in out of the rain, or wander off and forget how to get home, although they never did when younger. Be aware of this potential loss of mental acuity and see to it that your dog is not left in situations that could prove dangerous to him.

Your dog's sense of balance also will diminish as he gets older. A dog who has slept on your bed his whole life may one day lose his balance and fall off, a problem made more serious due to the fact his bones are more brittle as he ages. Two thick L.L. Bean polyester-fill dog beds placed one on top of the other next to your bed will be an acceptable substitute to most dogs used to the privilege of sleeping on your bed. It is high enough to be near you, yet not so high that the dog is likely to fall off it.

Every once in a while an old dog will revert to his youthful playfulness. He may try to scoot (tuck his tail end down and run) or lower his front end in a dog's universal "Let's play!" stance. Encourage him in this; let him know you still think him fun to play with.

Old dogs, as they grow deaf, find that they are not corrected verbally (as far as they can tell—they cannot hear you saying "No!" to them). They may therefore try out patterns of behavior that they never tried in the past, such as swiping food from the table. It is best to remove the situation (keep the dog away from unattended food-laden tables) rather than to correct the dog too much. A very old dog must not be spanked with a jumping bat or even with your hand; you could injure him. The most you should do is gently swat the front of his nose (against his nostrils) with the palm of your hand. But because a dog who has spent a lifetime responding to your verbal commands will not readily adjust to this new type of correction in advanced age, it is best just to keep him from situations in which he is likely to err.

Medical problems arise and can become serious much more rapidly in an old dog than in a young one. At the first sign of trouble, see a veterinarian. Don't delay; in an old dog it could be fatal. (See "Illness: Warning Signs.")

Serious illness is not an automatic death sentence for a dog, however. I had a dog for four years (on daily medication) after being diagnosed with Cushing's syndrome and a dog with cancer lived out his life happily for three more years. Dogs are perfectly capable of choosing their own time to leave life. In my view, the decision should be left to them; it's their life. It seems to me that euthanasia for dogs is often really an attempt by human beings who feel helpless in the face of serious or incurable illness, to "do something to take charge of things." I'm not sure this is right. Dogs see the question of quality of life differently from us. If they can enjoy *something* in the present—a pat, a comforting word, a body hug, a hand-fed treat—they focus on and enjoy that. I don't think they worry about the future much. Old dogs need time to think about their life, and I think it unfair to deprive them of this time because we human beings are unhappy that they are sick or old.

See "Death of a Dog."

OVERWEIGHT DOGS

An overweight dog is an unhealthy dog. No matter how much he may love to eat, no matter how cute and chubby the dog may appear to be, an owner does a dog no kindness by allowing him to become overweight. A dog's ribs should be felt easily just beneath his skin; if he feels "padded" or "squishy" against his ribs, he is overweight.

Like most training problems, an overweight dog is more a problem caused by a human being than it is a problem caused by a dog. The attitude of the human being must be corrected; some people have as much trouble keeping their dogs on a sensible diet as they do keeping themselves on one.

An overweight dog suffers stress on all his organs, and carrying around extra pounds places stress on his joints and back. It puts strain on his breathing. It makes him sluggish.

The solution is to feed less food, use a low-fat formula (many low-fat or "senior" formulas are available at pet stores), and increase the amount of exercise the dog gets. (See "Bicycle Riding with Your Dog.") Exercise performs two functions: It burns calories, and it causes the *rate* at which the dog's metabolism burns these calories to speed up, so the dog burns calories faster. If you must feed snacks between meals, feed raw carrots or broccoli. If your dog is truly starving, he will eat them. If he rejects them, he is just holding out for a fat-producing treat; ignore him.

Note: Some diseases can cause a dog to appear overweight when the problem is altogether different. Cushing's syndrome, a hormone imbalance correctable with treatment, can cause a bloated, extended, and "saggy" stomach. Thyroid underactivity can also cause a dog to put on weight. If in any doubt, consult your veterinarian.

PENS AND FENCED ENCLOSURES

A fenced-in yard or enclosure where your dog can play and run around is a great convenience to both you and your dog. It makes both canine and human lives so much easier that I highly recommend that you build such an area if at all possible.

The fence must be high enough that your dog cannot jump it. For very small dogs (Chihuahua, Maltese, short-legged terriers weighing ten pounds or so), a four-foot fence may be high enough. If your dog is of medium size or very athletic, you must increase the fence height to five or even six feet. If your dog shows any tendency to try to climb or jump out of even this, the only prevention is to attach an addition at the top, slanted upward and inward at an angle all around the fence.

All dogs can dig. Some take real pleasure in the activity. You must therefore bury at least six inches to a foot of fence in the ground to make certain your dog cannot dig his way out. Some dogs, of course, will not make the attempt, but owners of even lazy and placid dogs have sometimes been surprised to find a hole under the fence and their dog missing.

The gate needs a padlock so neighborhood children cannot leave it open by accident. An easy arrangement is to slip a choker collar, available at any pet store, through the fencepost and the post of the gate, and fasten it with the padlock. Use a lock made for outdoor use (it won't rust) that has a combination so you won't need to find a key every time you want to go through the gate. Under the gate, bury bricks so the dog cannot dig out here.

Types of fence that work well include chain-link (for large, strong dogs) or turkey wire (square holes about $1\frac{1}{2} \times 2$ inches in size), with medium-gauge wire strong enough to hold most medium-size dogs. Chickenwire is of too fine a gauge to hold up if even a small dog wants to get through it. Solid wooden fences ("stockade fence") prevent dogs from having a view. Stockade fences also are prone to develop holes at the bottom where a dog can push his way out, so they aren't the best choice.

Be sure there is shade, water, and a dry place to lie down out of the rain within the pen. If there is a doghouse, check the bed for dampness periodically.

The most satisfactory ground surface I have found is a base of six inches of sand with a surface of small, smooth round pebbles slightly smaller than a pencil eraser in size. The sand allows urine to drain away, leaving not even a smell behind, and the pebbles provide a surface less prone to be tracked continually into your house on your dog's—and your own—feet. A good rain or a hosing down makes the surface like new.

If you keep a garbage pail with a plastic liner and tight-fitting lid, a shovel, and a stick handy in the pen, cleanup of solid waste is simple and convenient.

PESTICIDES, EXTERMINATORS, INSECT SPRAYS FOR THE HOUSE

Exterminators who spray your house for termites, insects, and pests such as ants or, in cities, roaches, kill these pests with poisons. Dogs are vulnerable to poisons that settle on the floor, where the soles of their feet can absorb them, and where they can lick the residue off their feet. Dogs also may sniff or lick in cracks and crannies along walls where exterminators have sprayed.

Therefore, it is safer for your dog (and other pets) if you use ant traps, roach traps, and other noninvasive procedures rather than having exterminators spray in your house.

Be certain that you place any such traps in places where no dog or cat can reach them. Even a small amount of poison can kill or seriously harm a pet. Dogs, like small children, will play with and try to chew open insect traps. Put them on a shelf where no pet can climb.

If you *do* use a professional exterminator, be sure all dishes for food and water are removed before he sprays the house. The residue left on your dog's dishes can make him sick.

A dog who eats poison or absorbs it through his feet may go into shock. He will appear stunned, listless, or behave erratically, pacing and shaking. Immediately take a pet showing symptoms like these to a veterinarian.

It goes without saying that if your house is sprayed by an

exterminator, *all* pets must be out of the house at the time of treatment, and for several hours afterward. Anything that breathes must be removed prior to spraying—dogs, cats, hamsters, gerbils, fish, birds, reptiles.

PILLS: FEEDING THEM TO YOUR DOG THE EASY WAY

There are two ways to feed pills and medicines to your dog.

The hard way is to stand over your dog, pry open his jaws with your hands, hold his mouth open while tipping his head up toward the ceiling, stuff the pills as far down into his throat as you can, hold his mouth shut with your hand, and stroke his throat with the other hand until he swallows the pills.

The easy way is to wrap the pills in cream cheese and let your dog eat them. If he shows any hesitation, give him some plain cream cheese (without pills in it) to allow him to develop a taste for it. When he eagerly awaits the next ball of cheese, put a pill inside it. Dogs seldom chew anything, so he probably will swallow the cheese ball and pill in a gulp, especially if you make it small enough to just cover one pill at a time.

Other useful disguises for pills include raw ground beef and cat food (the kind that balls up neatly and is sticky enough to hold the pills inside).

Note: Certain medicines must be given *without* food. Check with your veterinarian.

POOPER SCOOPERS

It may not be your favorite part of dog walking, but the law that says we must pick up after our dogs is a good one. Think of it as insurance that benefits you and your dog by keeping the streets and parks cleaner and more healthful. At worst, picking up your dog's feces is a task that occupies approximately a mere six seconds of each day.

One of the easiest and cheapest ways to deal with the matter is to persuade your supermarket or greengrocer to sell you a full roll of plastic bags of the type fruit comes in. These will last the average dog almost a year and cost somewhere between $7 and $12, depending on where you live. You put your hand into a clean bag, pick up the dog waste (the plastic prevents your actually touching it, of course), and turn the bag inside out in one simple motion. You can then knot the top of the bag and drop it into a trash can. These bags fit easily into your pocket, taking up practically no room.

If you prefer, you can buy a pooper scooper at a pet store. They come in various models, most of which work well. Their disadvantage is that they force you to carry a cumbersome piece of equipment whenever you walk your dog.

SALT ON SIDEWALKS

Many cities sprinkle salt on sidewalks and roadways at the first sign of a snowflake. This coarse salt, approximately the size of a pea, causes sharp pain to a dog's feet when it makes contact with the dog's pads. The problem becomes more troublesome after snow begins to melt, and the salty solution runs everywhere.

If your dog suddenly picks up one or more paws in obvious distress, cries, or tries to lick his feet while you are walking over sidewalks that have been salted, the cause is probably salt. If there is uncontaminated snow or water available, scrape his feet gently in it to remove the cause. If this is not possible, wash his feet off in the bathtub or dip them in a can filled with warm water as soon as you return home.

Dogs hate the pain, which is acute while it lasts. But it will do no lasting damage, as long as you are careful to wash the salt off.

You might want to consider getting together with other people to discourage overuse of salt in your town or city. Some towns have banned its use—it pollutes the water table—and returned to use of snow shovels instead.

SHEDDING (HAIR)

All dogs shed hair, even those like poodles that are said to be nonshedding. Some shed more than others, and if the hair color contrasts with that of your furniture, rugs, or clothing, it can seem worse than it actually is.

Two things will help: First, brush your dog daily. If his coat is long, use a brush that will not hurt him. Some of the best brushes have bristles like a hairbrush for people, made of synthetic material and fairly flexible. You also can try a brush with metal bristles set in a flexible rubber base, which tends to minimize pulling on the dog's sensitive skin when you brush.

With short-haired dogs, use a brush or a shedding blade, which is a strip of steel about a foot long and an inch or two wide with serrated edges on one side. Shedding blades stimulate the dog's skin and remove loose hair at the same time. They don't work very well on long-haired dogs, such as collies. You can buy them at pet stores or riding goods shops. (They are used on horses too.)

By grooming your dog daily, you remove loose hair that would otherwise end up on your clothes or furniture. It also gives you a chance to examine your dog for cuts, scrapes, lumps, and bumps you otherwise might not notice.

The second thing that will help the problem of shedding is to use a lint and hair remover on clothes. This looks like a roll of tape on a handle, which is exactly what it is. You roll the tape roller over your clothing, and hair stuck to your clothes sticks instead to the tape surface of the roller. Then you peel off the used tape, and a fresh surface is ready for use again. You can buy these rollers in vets' offices, pet supply stores, and even some dry cleaners' shops.

Note: If your dog sheds hair in what appears to be an excessive or abnormal manner, such as a thinning of the hair on his back or sides, the problem is probably medical and needs the attention of a veterinarian. A number of conditions can cause excessive hair loss including Cushing's syndrome (a hormonal imbalance), parasites (fleas, ticks, lice, mites), ringworm (actually a fungus growth), hyperthyroidism (overactive thyroid), and other causes.

SHOPPING WITH YOUR DOG

In most cities, in towns, and even in some malls, you can take your dog with you when you go shopping. (However, if you are asked not to, under no circumstances leave your dog, even for a moment, tied up outside while you go into a store. [See "Dognapping."]) If no one objects, and you like to shop with your dog for company, be sure to observe these safety rules.

- *Escalators:* Absolutely *never* take a dog on an escalator unless you can pick him up and carry him the whole time you are on it. The dog's feet can be caught and pulled into the mechanism of the machine, grinding them to ribbons. Many people do not realize how extremely dangerous escalators are to any dog.
- *Revolving doors:* If you must enter through revolving doors, do *not* take your dog along—unless, again, you can pick him up easily. (See "Doors: Double, Revolving, Elevator.")
- *Changing booths:* Take your dog into the changing room with you. Never leave your dog tied outside the door or anywhere else for even a moment. Don't believe that "no one can touch my dog, because he's so well trained or so much a one-person dog"—a dog thief can take *any* dog.

Keep your dog in "heel" position and do not allow him to bother other shoppers.

SIT! (SIT ON COMMAND)

Be sure your dog is wearing his choker collar. Attach a four-foot leash to the ring. If you are not sure how to do this, see "Collars."

Take the dog to a quiet area in a room or yard, where there will be no distractions. Face in the same direction as your dog. With your right hand, grasp the leash about a foot from the dog's collar. Stand beside the dog and, with your fingertips (not the palm of your hand), press down on his back just above the tail. At the same time pull straight upward with the leash with your other hand. This has the effect of a seesaw: As one end goes up, the other end goes down.

When the dog sits, stop both signals and praise him verbally. Do not pat him, because this action may distract him so much that he will stand up again. You want him to remain in the sit position for about ten seconds. Just say one time "Good dog!" and then repeat the command "Sit!" over and over for the entire time he is sitting. This reinforces the command.

Keep your right hand ready to pull upward on the leash and your left hand ready to press down on his tail end with your fingertips in case he forgets and stands up.

When he has been in sit position for about ten seconds, stand next to the dog (you stand on the right, he sits at your left facing forward), then walk forward a few steps and stop. Repeat the exercise ten times in a row, then praise him with hugs and pats, and leave the lesson until another day.

If your dog refuses to sit when you pull up on his leash while pushing down on his back end with your fingertips, try pushing down with more force. If this does not work, place your whole arm around his back end, with your elbow just above his hocks (the bend in the hind legs). Push inward so you move his hind legs in the direction of his front end, until he is forced to sit. At the same time, pull upward with your right hand on the leash.

Sit! Teaching Your Dog to Sit on Command
Pull straight up on the leash with one hand as you push down on the dog's back near the tail with the other.

SNACKS AND TREATS

It is certainly not cruel to feed your dog at mealtimes only—either once or twice a day—and give him no snacks or between-meal treats at all. This has the advantage of insuring that your dog's diet will be balanced, as long as you feed a good-quality dog food containing essential nutrients. (See also "Dog Food.") It also insures that your dog will not look for handouts all day long. But if you want to feed your dog between-meal snacks, be sure that they are healthful ones and that you do not substitute poor-nourishment treats for his regular meals.

My own policy is to feed raw vegetables such as carrots, broccoli and cabbage for between-meal snacks. If you have two or more dogs, this will probably work; they become competitive. ("It may be only a raw carrot, but if I don't eat it, Fred will get it.")

Prepared dog biscuits usually are not as nutritious as regular dog food. They are made to be tasty and most dogs love them, but beware of giving them in place of properly balanced dog food. Many brands have a high concentration of fat and sugar.

If your dog gains weight (see "Overweight Dogs"), the first thing you should cut down on is snacks, unless you feed only raw vegetables, which cannot put weight on a dog.

SPAYING/NEUTERING

Spaying (for females) and neutering (for males) prevents dogs from reproducing. It also greatly decreases or prevents the chances of your dog's dying from breast cancer or prostate cancer. Spaying or neutering tends to bring out an even-tempered personality. And with all the dogs coldly killed daily by so-called animal shelters, due to our failure to cut down breeding, altering your dog certainly makes good sense. If you really need convincing, ask your local shelter to see the dogs they intend to destroy in that day alone, because there are no homes for them. It may just break your heart.

Spaying removes the ovaries from the female by surgical means. Your dog will be hospitalized for a full day or perhaps overnight. Be sure not to allow the dog any food or water for twelve hours prior to surgery, as an anesthetized dog can vomit and choke to death if he has eaten or drunk water prior to unconsciousness.

Neutering removes the testicles of a male dog. Because these are located in a sac outside the dog's body, the procedure is simpler than spaying. The same rules apply prior to anesthesia.

If you are longing for a puppy, think twice before breeding your dog. Why not consider giving a home to an already existing puppy? You could save a life, and the mystery of life is just as great in a puppy you didn't breed as one you do.

Every dog pictured in this book was found on the streets or in city dumps, or dog pound shelters, and would be dead except that they were taken in as strays. Two or three of them are purebred dogs, the others mixed breeds. Breeders argue that there is a need for well-bred dogs and that they fill this need. But it is indisputable fact that many of the dogs bred by even responsible breeders die. Some are purchased by irresponsible owners, later to get loose or be dumped when the owners don't know how to train them, some end up in shelters which put to death *millions* of dogs each year. There are an estimated 12 dogs for each available owner. This means 11 will die. How can anyone in good conscience bring more dogs into the world when so many cannot find homes as it is? This is my view, and it is sure to find argument with breeders and puppy mill breeders (who breed indiscriminately, selling in huge volume to pet shops). I believe that until a *truly* humane solution to overpopulation and abandonment of dogs (and other animals) is achieved—and not by killing them off when they become inconvenient or too numerous—we owe it to dogs to have them spayed or neutered.

News flash: As of this writing, the Humane Society of America has "asked" all breeders to declare a moratorium on all breeding of dogs for one year. This at least marks an important recognition of the source of the problem, although I have doubts as to its effectiveness. But spaying and neutering greatly help by preventing yet more puppies in an already flooded market.

SPITE

Spite is akin to sulkiness; sulkiness, if improperly handled, can lead to spiteful behavior. (See "Sulking.")

Spite consists of behavior that your dog knows full well is wrong, for which he knows he will be punished. But he thinks it is better to be punished than to miss an opportunity to make very clear to you that he dislikes something you are doing. Often the feelings motivating a dog to spiteful behavior are interwoven with feelings of jealousy. (See "Jealousy of Another Pet or Person.")

A typical and common example of a dog showing spite is one who waits until you have gone to work, then goes to your bed and urinates right in the middle of it. Your dog is saying "I don't like the fact you have gone off and left me here all alone, and I'll punish you for that," or "I don't like the fact that you allow your husband (or wife) to sleep here, when *I* would like to sleep here, so I'll pee on his (her) side of the bed and show you how much I don't approve of your selfish behavior." Or a dog who is on a diet and is fed a smaller meal than he feels entitled to may chew up his food dish. ("I'll show them; if they intend to starve me, I'll demolish my dish.")

Deal with spite crisply and coldly. Do not be confused or moved by your dog's point of view; don't feel sorry for him. If the dog has urinated on the bed, put a leash on him, drag him to the spot, hold him as near it as possible, yell "No!" and give two or three sharp swats with your jumping bat (see p. 140) on the dog's thigh. Another effective method of correction with some dogs is to throw bomber snaps on the bed. (See "Aggression with People.") Don't attempt to correct the dog without having him on a leash; some dogs may try to bite if you do. As soon as you have corrected him, take him off the bed, lead him to another part of the house or apartment, and let him loose again. Ignore him. He will probably hide for a while, then come to you demanding attention. Give him an absentminded pat, but do not make a fuss over him. On the other hand, do not continue to scowl at him or continue to show disapproval. Your disapproval must be shown only while you correct him (with the jumping bat or bomber snaps).

Under no circumstances continue to punish a dog by locking him in a small room, depriving him of dinner, tying him up on a short leash, or verbally punishing him. Once the correction is over, let it be *completely* over. It is important for your dog to distinguish between his doing an unacceptable action (peeing on the bed) and his being an unacceptable, unlovable dog (one that you continue to punish after he already got the message).

Never make him feel you don't like him; merely show him clearly that you won't accept certain unacceptable actions on his part.

STAY! (STAY IN PLACE ON COMMAND)

If your dog understands thoroughly the commands for sit and down (see "Sit!" and "Down!"), you really don't need the stay command. Once you place him in sit or down position, he should remain in that position until commanded otherwise.

However, many people prefer to use the stay command. Here is how to teach it.

Place your dog in the sit position. Say "Stay!" Briefly place the palm of your hand against his nose. Walk away from the dog five or six feet. If he moves even a little bit, go back to the dog, lift his leash, give a sharp jerk upward on it, and, with your right hand, smack his nose with the flat of your hand against his nostrils.

Again, repeat the command "Stay!" and walk away. When the dog has remained motionless for fifteen seconds, go back to his side (do not call him to you), pick up his leash, and give the command "Heel!" Move forward ten feet, and repeat.

When he obeys perfectly, add temptations, such as slices of sausage or something else your dog likes a great deal to eat. Place these on the ground a few feet from your dog. If he lunges for the temptations, knowing full well he is supposed to remain in the stay position, use your jumping bat on his thigh to administer two or three sharp swats, hard enough to sting, and repeat the exercise. This makes it worth the dog's while to choose to obey your command rather than yield to temptation.

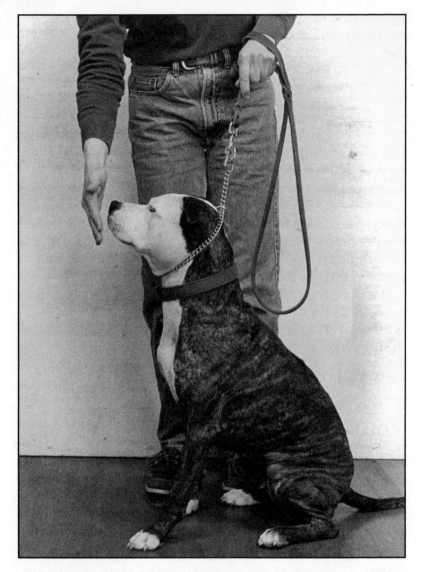

Stay! (Stay in Place on Command)
*Briefly place the palm of your hand against
the dog's nose before moving away from him.*

When the dog has accomplished the exercise, gather up all the temptations and store them in the refrigerator. Do not feed them to the dog. In this way you will teach him that there is no advantage to looking for treats on the ground (this could save his life, incidentally—see "Eating Food from the Street") and will make him less inclined to try to grab treats rather than remain in the stay position.

STRESS

Dogs suffer from stress just as human beings do. Prolonged stress takes a toll on a dog's health. Stress upsets the normal balance of your dog's hormones, nervous system function, heartbeat, and breathing rates. It can cause a dog to decline in condition and body weight, to lack concentration, or to go into a depression. Stress can be caused by parasites, bacteria, or virus infection, trauma (as from a dog fight or injury to a limb), burns, breeding, being taken to too many dog shows, or the withholding of affection.

All stress is not bad. Stress caused by the tension of a dog's waiting for you to throw the ball so he can retrieve it is good stress—the dog goes into "high alert" as he watches you, waiting for you to throw the ball. Then, as he runs after the ball, the built-up stress is released: This kind of stress—*stress that has an answer*—is beneficial.

Stress that *has no answer* is harmful, however. Unless the dog can see something he can do to change the situation (such as retrieving the ball in the example just given), stress becomes a trigger for anxiety. A dog in this "burned out" condition is vulnerable to physical and emotional disease.

The question of stress is a complex one, because so many causes trigger stress reactions, and different dogs respond very differently to the same stimuli. A nervous-natured dog may be upset by rowdy children, continuous noise, or lack of hugs and attention, while a placid-tempered dog may welcome rowdy children as entertainment, not pay any attention to a noisy environment, and sleep peacefully until someone remembers to pat him.

A stressed-out dog can have fewer red blood cells than normal. Because these cells carry vital oxygen to the dog's organs and all his body tissues, this diminishing of red blood cells can have far-reaching implications. Feeding your dog increased protein may help offset the lack. But to a dog whose life is stressful the only really satisfactory remedy is to remove the stress or at least minimize it until it does not cause anxiety.

Some causes of stress include:

- *Noise* that the dog is unable to get away from.
- *Indignity:* Being made to sleep in the garage or outdoors when used to sleeping on the master's bed; or being made to wear a dog coat that the dog finds offensive, for example.
- *Travel:* Changing conditions, unfamiliar situations, heat or cold.
- *Heat,* especially direct sunlight from which the dog is unable escape; also *cold,* with no way of warming up.
- Being left in a *boarding kennel.*
- *Breeding,* and especially breeding too often.
- *Dog shows,* especially if too often.
- *Lack of affection,* especially if your dog is used to hugs and pats and talking.
- *Fleas,* eczema, ringworm, ear mites, "hot spots."
- *Dogfights.*
- *Teasing* by passersby if your dog's fenced pen is vulnerable to this.

- *Lack of exercise,* being cooped up too long in a crate or pen.
- *Illogical demands* from human beings; being allowed to get up on furniture one time, then being punished for it the next; being punished for medically caused incontinence that the dog has no control over.
- *Separation anxiety,* especially in abused dogs with new owners they have grown to love and trust.

It is evident when a dog is stress-free or enjoys only the beneficial sort of stress. He is alert, cheerful, playful, his eyes shine, his coat is glossy. If your dog appears dull, listless, sad, or lacks energy, first have a competent veterinarian give him a thorough workup to try to find the cause if it is medical. If this turns up nothing significant, the dog may well be suffering from stress. Try to see things from his perspective. You are his only chance at a happy and fulfilled life. Treat a dog as you would a cherished human companion; be considerate of his need for a reasonable schedule of feeding, walks, and companionship. When you are with your dog, give him "quality time" so he feels he is the total center of attention for the time you are with him.

Dogs treated fairly and with love give back a hundred times over what is given to them. Be worthy of this gift.

SULKING

Some dogs are prone to sulk when they cannot get their own way. If you decide that your dog must stay in another room when you have guests who are allergic to dogs, for instance, a sulky-natured dog will lower his tail, look balefully at you, and skulk away into the corner of the room you banish him to rather than go cheerfully.

Dogs who sulk are often inadvertently encouraged by their humans, who respond to their droopy, sad-seeming behavior by giving them added attention and comfort. This is exactly what you should *not* do; it merely encourages dogs in their sulkiness. It teaches them that in order to get a great deal of attention from you, all they need to do is act sulky and spoiled.

When you deal with a sulking dog, be brisk, matter-of-fact, and accomplish in the minimum time what you want to do (such as putting your dog in a spare room while guests visit). Ignore completely your dog's sulking. When he sees that it has no effect on you, he will stop the behavior or at least tone it down.

TEETH: BRITTLENESS AND CLEANING

If your dog's teeth break or chip, especially if the dog is older, find a veterinarian who takes a holistic or "whole-dog" approach. Brittle teeth are a sign that something is not right with your dog's general health. Vitamin and mineral supplements may help. One of the best vitamins is Canine Plus, sold only through veterinarians. Beware of many of the more "popular" brands of dog vitamins sold at pet stores. They amount to little more than a pleasant snack for your dog and have little value as a supplement.

Good, strong, white teeth are generally a sign of excellent overall health. Your dog's teeth are like your own in that they must be kept free of tartar (the brownish layer that accumulates toward the top of the tooth near the gums). Failure to remove tartar can cause cavities, tooth loss, and gum disease. (See also "Bad Breath.")

If you begin gradually, you will be able to teach your dog to allow you to scrape the tartar off his teeth yourself. This saves the expense of having a vet do it for you. It is also safer, as most vets will not undertake the procedure unless they put the dog under anesthesia.

To teach your dog to allow his teeth to be cleaned, you will need a sharp, hard tool like an awl, available at hardware stores. If you can get someone with a home woodworking shop to bend its very tip over, your job will be even easier. You also can use a knife or scissors, if you are careful.

First, take your dog on a long walk or bike ride. (See "Bicycle Riding with Your Dog.") This will tire him out and relax him. Then feed him, so he will be even more contented.

Then put him on a comfortable surface, a rug or dog-bed on the floor or on a chair (if you allow him on furniture) where you have good bright light that will let you see his teeth clearly. Gently pull up the lip so the canine ("fang") tooth is exposed.

With your tool, *very gently* scrape the tooth, being careful not to touch the gum. You are not trying actually to remove tartar at this point; you are only getting the dog used to the process. Do four or five scrapes along the tooth, then praise the dog and let him go. Repeat the process several times a day. When he is convinced that nothing bad will happen, he will allow you to press down hard enough on the tooth to remove actual tartar. Tartar flakes off in small chips if you scrape at it with sufficient pressure.

Be very careful never to let the tool touch the gums accidentally. If it slips and cuts his gum, a dog will have real reservations about letting you try the procedure again.

If your dog shows any signs of aggressiveness toward people (see "Aggression with People"), do not attempt to clean his teeth yourself. The aggression problem must be thoroughly solved first.

When you have removed the tartar from the inside and outside surfaces of the canine teeth, begin on the other teeth, one by one. Be sure to do the molars all the way at the back, which collect tartar more than many other teeth and are often overlooked.

The best plan is to do a *little* at a time, not try to complete the whole job at once. That way the dog learns that while it may not be his favorite way of spending time, it doesn't hurt, and it only lasts for a little while.

TICKS

There are many varieties of ticks. In general, the larger ticks are brown and flat until engorged with blood, and easily visible due to their larger size. They cause blood loss, anemia, and sometimes even paralysis. A small variety, less than one-quarter the size of the larger tick, can cause a serious disease called Lyme disease, which can result in joint pain, arthritic changes, and even death.

Fortunately, you can prevent complications from ticks by carefully examining your dog throughout the months ticks thrive, in spring and summer and early fall. If you find a tick, dab rubbing alcohol or peroxide on it, then grasp it with a tissue or tweezers and pull it slowly straight out away from the dog. Even if the head of the tick comes off, it will not harm the dog or, contrary to common lore, grow back.

Tick dips are useful in cases of extreme infestation. But remember that such chemicals are poisons, and prevention is better in the long run.

Flea and tick collars, in my experience, do little good. The plastic kind (generally white in color) are impregnated with chemicals that are supposed to kill or repel fleas and ticks for several months. This kind of collar carries a warning that it should not be used if the dog is wet or harm may result. If you do want to try one, they are available in pet stores and supermarkets. Use according to directions printed on the package.

A better choice might be an electronic flea collar, which reportedly drives away ticks and fleas by emitting an ultra-high sound that dogs and people cannot hear but fleas find intolerable. These cost about $20 and are advertised in the back of pet magazines, such as *Dog Fancy*. Some people have reported reasonably good results. But a thorough daily visual check for ticks is the best defense. A garlic and yeast supplement added to your dog's food, called Hop-off, is available from some vets. After several weeks it builds up in the oil of the coat. It must therefore be used with a special shampoo that does not strip the oils from a dog's coat. The shampoo is called Sho-off. Call (215) 493-0621 for information if you cannot buy these products from your local vet.

Avon Skin So Soft (mix 10 oz. water with 1 oz. Avon) sprayed lightly on dogs is nontoxic and repels fleas well.

TRAVEL WITH YOUR DOG

Travel with your dog for long distances can be difficult and risky. In general, it is best to leave your dog in a reliable kennel when you go on trips. (See "Boarding Kennels.")

But sometimes travel is unavoidable, as when you are moving to a different part of the country or out of the country. In such cases, caution and careful preparation are the keys to successful transportation of your dog.

Even short trips—across a city, for example, to reach a vet—present problems. Luckily, most travel methods have been thoroughly "field tested" by thousands of other dog owners over the years. Here are some of the methods you may want to consider in the event you must travel with your dog, either locally or long distance.

BY AIRPLANE

Dogs can be shipped either as *cargo* or as *excess baggage* on commercial airlines. If shipped excess baggage, typical costs are about $50 to 100 to Germany from New York City. Using this method, you are charged twice the normal excess baggage charge and are charged by the piece. (One dog equals one piece.) Some airports charge additional fees; for example, JFK charges a $50 "livestock fee" plus a $10 fee for "typing airway bill."

If you ship your dog as cargo, you are charged by a complicated formula: the volume of the dog's kennel (length × height × width) divided by 166 multiplied by 110 percent of the normal cargo rate. Confirm with airlines in writing what this works out to in dollar costs.

In either case, you will need to provide a container with good ventilation on all four sides. (See illustration in section on "Crates.") If you do not have ventilation on all sides of the crate and the cargo shifts during flight, your dog's air can be cut off and he can suffocate. A careless airline employee also could load your dog's container next to other freight without being sure to leave adequate ventilation. Having ventilation screens on all four sides multiplies your chances of good ventilation.

The container must be big enough for the dog to turn around in and to stand up in with a minimum of two inches above his head. Shipping crates differ from normal crates in that they are of polyurethane (plastic), with grates for ventilation in the upper part of the walls and on the front entrance door. You can buy one at large pet supply stores. Be sure you get the strongest, sturdiest one you can to avoid possibility of crushing.

Lock the crate when your dog is in it with a strong padlock. (The kind with a combination is best so you won't have to search for a key in an emergency.) Be sure to write down the combination number on your passport or driver's license where you can find it easily if you forget it.

You will need to provide veterinary records of DHLPP vaccinations and rabies innoculation. (See "Vaccinations.") If you fail to do this, the airline or the customs officials in the country you go to can destroy your dog.

If shipping abroad, be certain to contact in advance the embassy of every country you will pass through or enter. *Ask for all requirements and restrictions, in writing.* This is critical; failure to do so can cause great difficulty later. For instance, if you are changing planes in London, and due to delays that are no fault of your own you must stay more than forty-eight hours, your dog will be impounded and kept in quarantine for the next *six months.* In addition, you will be charged the equivalent of about $40 if your dog's crate is moved from one airplane to another for the next leg of the journey.

You may want to consider sedating your dog prior to a trip of some length. Discuss this fully with your veterinarian. Also include a water device (similar to those for hamsters, only much bigger). Be sure your dog has at least a quart of water for a twelve-hour trip for a medium-size dog. Provide a small quantity of dry dog food in a small bowl attached to the inside of the door of the crate. Both devices are available at pet supply stores.

The livestock cargo cabin usually is located directly beneath the passenger cabin. Airlines "guarantee" that it is properly pressurized and heated.

However, there are horror stories, which are well documented, of dogs arriving dead due to decompression of the cargo cabin, shifting of cargo that blocks off air, and lack of heat. Dogs have gotten loose on the runway of the airport during an airplane change, dogs have been shipped to the wrong country by mistake, and dogs have been lost with no trace.

Only a blind person can legally take a dog with him in the passenger cabin. I know of at least one person who bought a seeing-eye harness, taught his dog to walk with it, and took his dog in the seat next to him. (He had to pay for the seat.) The only difficulty he experienced was when the movie came on and he had to pretend he merely wanted to listen to it with the headphones.

Many people have shipped dogs safely on airlines. Most dogs arrive without incident. But there are a great number of factors in airline travel over which you have no control. There are risks. My own advice is do *not* ship a dog by air unless it is unavoidable.

BY CAR

Many dogs love to ride in cars. A few get hyperexcited, a few get frightened, and a few get carsick.

For dogs who love to travel in cars: Put an old sheet or blanket on the seat if your dog's nails will harm the surface. Open the window enough so your dog can get his nose but not his eyes out the window. (His eyes can be hurt if foreign objects, such as insects or sand, blow into them at high speeds.) Let him enjoy the smells outside as you drive. Do not drive with a dog in the front seat; even a well-behaved dog could interfere with your driving with disastrous results.

You can put a harness (available in pet shops) on your dog and attach the rear seat belt through it. Do *not* attach your dog by the collar to a seat belt, however; if you crash, you would break his neck. You can restrict the dog's movement by placing the leash in the jamb of the door so half of it is outside the car, closing the door with the leash caught in it. Be sure to tie the end of the leash outside the car into a loose knotted ball so it will not get caught on anything. One of the safest ways to travel by car with your dog is to put a crate in the back of a station wagon. (You also can fit a crate sideways in a sedan on the backseat.)

You can buy a fencelike divider that fits across the back section of a station wagon and prevents the dog from jumping into the backseat.

DANGER! In summer the temperature in a car, *even one with the windows open, can reach 112 degrees in two minutes. Never leave a dog in a parked car unless you are also in the car!* Dogs are prone to heatstroke. If you left your dog for five minutes while you ran into a store, with the car windows open for ventilation, you could come back to find your dog dead of heatstroke, a particularly horrible way to die. (Your dog could also be stolen if you do this; see "Dognapping.")

If your dog gets hyperexcited when you mention a car ride, the cure is to make as little of it as possible and to take him for short rides, around the block for example, as many times during the day as you can manage. If you do this for a week or two, even a hyperexcited dog eventually will see that car rides are not so thrilling as he formerly thought, since they are short and frequent and you seem to treat them as routine.

If your dog jumps around in the car, attach him by a harness to the backseat or put him in a crate when you drive.

If your dog is frightened of car rides (usually the result of some traumatic event before you got him, where someone hurt or confused him in or around a car), use the same correction as for hyperexcited dogs. Speak soothingly to him, and put down towels on the place where the dog will sit, as he may salivate heavily from fear.

For dogs who get carsick: The answer to the problem is to take the dog for very short rides as often as you can and to have an assistant hold the dog in his lap on the backseat in a position that insures that the dog's nose will be near an open window. (Open it only enough so the dog's nose, not his whole head, can stick out.) Keep large paper grocery bags handy in case the dog begins to get sick. These are large enough that most dogs won't mind putting their head into them. A plastic shopping bag outside the paper bag keeps it from leaking.

Do not let the dog eat or drink for at least an hour before taking him in a car.

If you must transport dogs who get carsick long distances, ask your veterinarian about Dramamine or Valium to make him "dopey" and get you through the crisis. But plan to take him on short trips as described earlier in order to correct the problem at its source, rather than merely to cover up the symptoms with drugs.

The American Automobile Association (AAA) provides a twenty-page free pamphlet on traveling with pets. Send a self-addressed stamped envelope to American Automobile Association, PR Department, 1000 AAA Drive, Heathrow, FL 32746-5063.

BY TAXI (HOW TO GET
A CAB TO STOP FOR YOUR DOG)

People with dogs living in cities face the problem of getting to a veterinarian with their dog using a cab, as most big-city dwellers do not own cars.

One of the most upsetting occurrences in stressful city life is to have a dog who must see a vet immediately, stand on a street corner with the sick dog, and watch taxi after taxi pass by. (It usually seems to be raining too.)

In an emergency, here is a ruse that often works. Given the choice between delaying help for a sick dog and pulling the wool over a taxi driver's eyes, I recommend fooling the driver and getting your dog to the vet without delay.

Here is how you do it: Make your dog sit in front of a car parallel-parked at the curb (be absolutely certain the parked cars both in front and behind you are empty.) Be sure he is out of sight from approaching taxicabs. Stand near the dog, but with your upper body clearly visible to the approaching cab driver. Hail the cab, remaining in front of the parked car so he must pull over to you, rather than going out to meet the cab yourself. When he stops, open the cab door, and unless he begins yelling at you that he refuses to take dogs, get into the cab *with* your dog.

Be especially careful at this stage; some drivers may attempt to drive away with your dog inside the cab before you can yourself get in. Try to *enter the cab at exactly the same time with your dog. Carry him into the cab if possible.*

Take a towel with you and assure the driver you will place it on the seat. Have a plastic bag which will fit easily into your pocket in case the dog gets carsick or defecates in the cab. Offer to pay extra; if the driver is merely an employee of a taxi fleet, he may not mind and will be glad of the extra bribe. If the taxi has a high partition between you and the driver, he may not even notice the dog at all, since he didn't see it when he drove up to you. In this case, just keep quiet about it; when you reach your destination, it won't be worth his while to berate you too much. If he was decent about it, leave a large tip.

The only exception, especially in large cities such as New York with populations from all over the world, is a taxi driver whose religious beliefs make him violently antidog. Such a person will not be moved by any considerations other than his own beliefs; do not argue with a driver who is adamantly against letting your dog into his cab. Just quietly try to find another.

BY SHIP

Travel by ocean liner is one of the safest ways to ship your dog long distance, especially if you are on hand to keep an eye on him.

Dogs shipped by oceangoing vessel need the same clearances as for shipping by air. (See "By Airplane.") Your dog will need to be brought onto the ship either in a crate or on a leash (check with the shipping line for instructions); he will be cared for and fed by ship's personnel assigned to this duty.

As with airline travel, you will need to contact the embassy of any country you will bring your dog into, in advance.

BY TRAIN

Train travel no longer allows you to have a dog in your roomette or compartment with you; if you travel by train your dog will be placed, in a crate, in the baggage car. The same problems can arise here that can arise in an airplane's cargo hold: lack of ventilation, lack of or excessive heat, accidental misrouting of your dog (someone misreads the label and puts him off at the wrong station). The advantage of travel by train is that you can go to visit your dog in the baggage compartment in most cases and keep an eye on him. Be present whenever the train stops so no one accidentally puts your dog off the train.

BY BUS

Unless your dog is small enough to fit into a bag carried over your shoulder, you probably will not be allowed to take him onto a public transport bus.

There is one ingenious exception to this, however. It won't work for everyone, but it works brilliantly for very strong people who have dogs with the right temperament.

I witnessed this on the streets of New York City: A young man, carrying a large soft-side zippered suitcase, was walking along the street. His other hand held the leash of his large, exuberant Irish setter. He came to a bus stop. He stopped, unzipped the suitcase, said pleasantly to the dog, "Hop in," and the dog sat neatly inside the suitcase, sideways, with his head slightly ducked but obviously quite content. The man zipped the suitcase up except for a small opening for air, picked up the case by the handle, and got onto the bus, and was driven away.

As he was about to get onto the bus, I had just enough time to ask him how he achieved such a neat solution to the problem of local bus travel with his dog. He said that from the time the dog was a puppy, he had trained him to sit in the case and that it had never presented any difficulty to either him or the dog.

Of course, if your dog is large, you will have to be strong

enough to lift him up the steps of a bus. But lifting a small or medium-size dog may not be beyond the capability of most people.

IN HOTELS/MOTELS

Some hotels and motels will allow dogs in your room with you. If you know where you plan to stay during your trip in advance, telephone or write them and ask their policy on dogs. Health laws vary from state to state; state, county, and city health laws govern whether pets may stay in public accommodations.

A list of hotels and motels across the country that will accept pets in your room with you is available from two sources, for a charge: *Take Your Pet USA,* Artco Publishing (Artco Offset, Inc.), 12 Channel Street, Boston, MA 02210, or from *Touring With Towser,* Quaker Professional Services, PO Box 9001 Suite 23-1, Chicago, IL 60604-9001.

In most states, common-law rules apply to pets in public places. Dogs may not be taken into rooms where food or drink are prepared, stored, or served, except in the case of dogs aiding the handicapped. Because the owner of the hotel/motel may be held responsible if a dog harms anyone on his premises, he is entitled to bar a dog from his property if he "believes it to be a danger" to his guests.

"Innkeeper laws" exist in all fifty states. Liability is determined state by state. The innkeeper is entitled to determine whether to allow pets in his hotel/motel or not. No law requires that he accept pets, but certain health laws may prohibit them. Each innkeeper establishes policy within the framework of his legal rights within the health code.

Some hotels, especially luxury hotels with long history of welcoming the pets of movie stars (in the 1930s and '40s everyone seemed to travel with a dog or two, from Basil Rathbone to Alfred Hitchcock) not only allow dogs for a nightly charge of $15 to $40, but will provide walking, feeding, and grooming services, and even turn down the dog's bed at night. (See books just cited for a list of hotels that welcome dogs.)

At any hotel/motel that accepts dogs as guests, you may be expected to pay a "reasonable fee," either a refundable damage fee (returned to you if your dog does not chew up the bedspreads or mess on the rug) or a nonrefundable "housekeeping fee" for the presumed extra work entailed in allowing your pet in the room with you. *Ask in advance* whether the money is refundable or not.

VETERINARIANS WHILE TRAVELING

You may not need a vet while traveling, but it pays to know in advance the address and telephone number of the major veterinary hospitals in cities you will visit. (See "Veterinarians.") Also ask friends in areas you will visit which vets they recommend.

TRICKS YOU CAN TEACH YOUR DOG

BEG!

Teaching your dog to beg is one of the times you will need a food incentive for most dogs. Take a small cube of cheese in one hand. Place your dog in the sit position. (See "Sit!") Hold the cheese just higher than the dog can reach while sitting. Say "Beg!"

If the dog tries to lift one or both front feet off the ground in an attempt to reach the cheese, give him the reward and get another piece of cheese.

Repeat the exercise until he lifts both front feet off the ground. If he will not do this, or if he attempts to stand up, make him sit, then hold the cheese above his nose with one hand while lifting one or both front feet gently off the floor with the other. Don't expect too much at first—just a little attempt on his part is enough for the dog to earn the reward.

Gradually try to get the dog to lift his own front feet off the floor without your having to grasp them with your hand. Try stepping very gently on his toes with your own foot.

Try always to give him the reward when he is momentarily in the beg position, and say the verbal command at the same moment you give him the reward.

CATCHING FOOD OFF DOG'S NOSE

To teach your dog to toss food off his nose into the air and catch it, first teach him to beg. (See "Beg.")

Place your dog in the beg position. Take a small cube of cheese and balance it on the end of your dog's nose. Hold his muzzle gently with one hand to encourage him to keep his head still and his nose level.

If he comes down from the beg position and sits, make him return to it. Then rebalance the cube of cheese on his nose.

After a couple of seconds, quickly remove your hand from his muzzle, as you say "Catch!" The dog will probably drop the cheese on the floor the first few times. Each time this happens, pick up the cheese before he can grab it and immediately toss it into the air so the dog will catch it. Repeat until he catches it in the air. Say "Catch!" each time you toss the cheese.

Then repeat the first part of the exercise. As the dog begins to understand that he must remain in the beg position and that he cannot have the cheese unless he catches it in the air, at some point he will figure out that it is quicker if he tosses the cheese in the air and catches it himself, eliminating you as intermediary. Praise him for every attempt he makes.

CLIMBING LADDERS

Some dogs like the challenge of climbing ladders. Use a ladder that cannot possibly move or fall. The kind with flat steps rather than round rungs is easier for a dog to learn to climb.

Take your dog on a leash in the heel position. Go to the ladder yourself and climb up three or four rungs, to show the dog how you climb up it. Then pull him over to it and encourage him by saying enthusiastically "Come on! Climb!" You will have to pull him up the first couple of steps by force until he learns how to do it; most dogs will hang back initially until they learn that they can manage the task.

Some dogs, pit bulls and poodles among them, are highly

Tricks You Can Teach Your Dog
Some dogs love climbing ladders . . .

. . . and going down the sliding board.

agile and love to climb. I have taken pit bulls up a ladder and down a sliding board the first time in their life, and they behaved as if they had done it forever, wagged their tails, and wanted to go again and again.

Some dogs do *not* like this trick. If your dog shows signs of being really frightened, don't continue. Go on to a trick he enjoys and teach him that instead.

CRAWLING

To teach your dog to crawl along the ground on his belly, you first must teach him two other commands: Come! and Down! (See "Come!" and "Down!") For this trick use both voice and hand signals.

Put your dog in the down position. Hold him down lightly with one hand on his back, step backward, and say "Here!" As he tries to get up, say "Down!" and then repeat "Here!" If he manages to crawl even a little bit while staying close to the ground, praise him and let him get up. Then repeat. Say "Crawl!" as he crawls forward.

With all tricks, keep things lighthearted and fun. Try for the proper effect, but if you don't get what you want, get just a little bit of the right reaction and praise. Gradually build up the number of crawl steps you can get from the dog.

HOOP JUMPING

A trick that is fun to teach and never fails to get applause from human audiences (dogs love this) is to teach your dog to jump through your arms when you form them into a hoop shape.

First, block off a doorway with a low barrier of about a foot in height. Make the barrier by putting a broomstick or other sturdy stick across the door in such a way that the dog cannot go underneath it or around it. This trick works best if you use food as incentive. Take small squares of cheese and lure your dog over the barrier. When he is in midair over the jump, say "Jump!" Praise him when he lands on the other side. Then make him jump back again. Repeat this ten or twelve times in a row, saying "Jump!" each time.

Next, stand over the jump. Hold your arms in a very large circle. Keep the circle very big, with your hands not meeting at the bottom, so as not to crowd the dog when he jumps. It may be easier at this stage to have an assistant lure him over with cheese, since your hands will be occupied in making the hoop. Make sure that your head is on the *far* side, away from the dog, and hold it up and out of the way so he will not hit your chin when he jumps through.

Gradually, close the hoop of your arms until your hands are touching. When the dog will jump through consistently, remove the broomhandle barrier. You now have a jumping trick dog.

Most dogs who have learned this trick will at this point try out a different response—running around or under the hoop just to see if that "works" instead. When this happens, grab the dog as he slips by, if possible. Go back to the previous step (set up the barrier, make a hoop over it with plenty of room for the dog to jump through your arms), and repeat this step two or three times. Then let it go for another day. Start the next day with a repeat of this step.

As soon as the dog understands the trick, stop giving him food as a reward and give him lavish praise and body hugs. If an admiring audience will clap and give him lots of attention, so much the better.

ROLL OVER!

To teach your dog to roll over, first teach him the command for Down. (See "Down!")

Place the dog in the down position. Then push him over on his side so that he lies flat on the ground, with one foreleg and

Hoop Jumping
This trick never fails to get applause from human audiences. Dogs who have a touch of the ham in them love to perform it.

one hindleg in contact with the ground. (The other set of legs will be suspended in the air.)

Grasp the two legs lying flat on the ground, one in each hand. Now roll the dog over on his back and onto his other side. As you do this, say "Roll over!" Praise him when he does the movement correctly, or when he allows you to roll him over.

Continue with the exercise until he readily rolls over himself on command.

SHAKE HANDS

First decide what command word(s) you plan to use. Some people use the word "Shake!" some use "Give me five!" and so forth.

Place your dog in the sit position. (See "Sit!") Using your command word at the same time, gently grasp your dog's right front paw in a firm but gentle handshake. Shake the paw gently as you repeat the word.

Most dogs will learn the trick readily. If it takes a while for your dog to learn to hold out his paw on command, simply reach out and grasp it as described until he finally volunteers the paw himself.

TROLLEY WIRES

An alternative to a fenced enclosure is a trolley wire.

Buy two cables from a pet store. Attach the longest cable between your back porch and a distant tree, or between two trees, or between a tree and your garage; find the best place for location of the trolley wire by determining where your dog would be safest and happiest. Choose two completely immovable objects to which you can attach the ends of the cable.

Attach the second cable to the first by means of the snap at either end. Some pet stores sell ready-made setups for trolley wires, which have a small pulley included. This makes it easier for the cable that attaches to the dog to slide along the other cable. Then snap the free end to your dog's collar. Walk with him at first to give him the idea of where he can go on the trolley wire. He will be able to move the length of the longer cable and also side to side as far as permitted by the second cable.

An alternative to getting two cables is to substitute a long piece of heavy-gauge wire (at least three times the strength and diameter of metal coathanger wire) for the longer cable. Such wire allows the second cable to slip along more easily. The disadvantage is that this wire is a little more difficult to attach because it has no snaps.

Never leave a dog unobserved on a trolley wire. (See "Dognapping.")

URINATION PROBLEMS: MEDICAL

If a normally housebroken dog suddenly begins to urinate in the house, there may be a medical reason. Indications that there may be medical problems include frequent urination in small amounts, excessive drinking and urination in very large amounts, blood in the urine, straining, and obvious signs of distress or pain.

If any of these problems occurs, see a veterinarian without delay. Some possible causes may, if left untreated, be fatal to your dog.

Among the possible problems are *bladder infections* (treatable with antibiotics), *cystitis* (a type of infection treatable with antibiotics), *bladder stones* (treatable by surgery or special diet that dissolves the stones; fatal if untreated), *Cushing's syndrome* (a tumor on pituitary gland or adrenal gland, causing hormone imbalance, treatable by carefully regulated doses of pills or an implant that automatically releases the correct amount of the medication), and *kidney failure* (often treatable with drugs, fatal if untreated).

Note: Young dogs, female puppies in particular, show submissive affectionate behavior by urinating. This is normal in puppies and young dogs (up to two or even three years). Often the dog or puppy will lie down on the ground, belly up, showing utter submission. Don't correct a dog for this behavior; simply try to keep an area near the door where the dog greets you bare of rugs, and clean up the urine with Nature's Miracle, available at pet supply stores and some veterinarians, which removes all trace of odor. (It dismantles the odor using the principle of enzyme reaction.)

Hormone imbalance in female dogs can cause uncontrolled urination. It can sometimes be treated very effectively with one of two drugs, the names of which, abbreviated, are PPA and DES. Ask your vet.

A temporary way of dealing with urination caused by incontinence in the house, if you have a male dog, is to fold a small terry cloth towel lengthwise, place a disposable diaper on it (one diaper cut in two works fine for most dogs, though a very large dog might need an entire diaper), and fasten the towel snugly around the dog's "waist" with a couple of safety pins at the top. For female dogs you will need to rig up your own arrangement, or you can buy a ready-made harness called "Piddle Pants" from a catalog company called Pedigrees, The Pet Catalog. Their telephone number is (716) 637-1431, address is Box 905, Brockport, NY 14420-0905. Piddle Pants are machine washable, are easily put on or taken off with a Velcro fastener, and have a vinyl liner to hold disposable pads, also available from the company.

It may be easier just to block off part of the house where the floor is bare, such as a kitchen, cover it with a thick layer of newspapers, and confine the dog to this area until the problem is cured.

Whatever you do, don't make a dog with a medical problem feel bad by scolding or showing disapproval. If the cause is medical, it isn't the dog's fault. Just clean up the papers as soon as they are wet, and take the dog out more frequently than usual.

Do *not* limit the water intake of a dog who is drinking too much. Poisons in the dog's system require extra water to wash them out, and limiting a sick dog's water intake could be fatal.

VACCINATIONS

An essential part of owning a dog is getting him properly vaccinated. Unless you do, you are almost sure to lose your dog to a preventable but fatal disease sooner or later.

When you get a new puppy, take him to your vet for a checkup immediately. The vet will give him his first inoculations at age six to eight weeks. The vet will tell you when to return for the follow-up shots that build the puppy's immunity. Be sure you follow the schedule; failure to do so may leave your puppy unprotected. Keep your puppy or dog away from other dogs, and places where other dogs have been, until his vaccination series is complete.

The essential inoculations are DHLPP and rabies vaccinations. DHLPP is actually five shots in one: distemper, hepatitis, leptospirosis, parainfluenza, and parvovirus. All diseases are deadly, all are preventable by vaccination. Leptospirosis is contagious to human beings. Rabies is also contagious to human beings. But it too is entirely preventable by vaccination.

Your vet will probably send you a reminder to return with your dog at the same time next year. But just in case, mark the date on your calendar yourself.

VETERINARIANS: HOW TO FIND A GOOD ONE

One of the best ways to find a good vet is by asking people with well-kept, healthy-looking dogs whom they recommend. You can look up breeders of dogs (call the American Kennel Club for names and numbers) and ask them. Also ask friends or neighbors whose dogs are healthy and happy which vets they like and which they do not.

Ask if the vet is *board certified* for any special procedures. If your dog needs an operation, for instance, be sure the vet is board certified *in that specialty*. Otherwise you may be dealing with a generalist without a great deal of experience in that specialty.

Any good veterinarian's office should be clean, smell clean, and be orderly. If the personnel seem reasonable and organized, able to find records easily, and pleasantly businesslike, these are all good signs. Avoid any office where the vet or his/her personnel are rude, coercive, or careless about records.

If you live near one of the large teaching hospitals, you have near you both an excellent resource and a potential danger. Such hospitals see more of every kind of disease and medical problem of dogs, and have more experience, through sheer numbers of canine patients dealt with each year than any smaller vet's office is likely to see.

What is important to remember, however, is that in these teaching hospitals young, inexperienced veterinary students are learning their trade. If your dog needs any surgical procedure, it is in your pet's best interests to make sure the hospital's board-certified veterinarian signs a statement stating that he or she will perform the operation entirely himself and will not allow veterinary students to do more than observe. Yes, vet students do have to learn how to perform surgery. But unless you want them to learn by practicing on your anesthetized pet, be sure the vet agrees in advance not to allow this, and get it in writing.

For most routine procedures, such as DHLPP and rabies vaccinations, your local vet is more convenient. But where the diagnosis seems more complex, it may pay to have a second opinion from one of the large hospitals in the nearest big city. *All* vets can and do make mistakes, so several opinions are much better than one for any serious or persistent condition. A dog of ours with hair loss and incontinence was diagnosed by three different vets as having a urinary tract infection; the fourth vet correctly diagnosed Cushing's syndrome. Similarly, another dog's severe itchiness was twice diagnosed as acute flea allergy (once by a leading veterinary hospital). It was a local vet who correctly diagnosed need for fatty acid supplements and antihistamines, which cured the condition after a full year of ineffective attempts. When in doubt, ask again.

WAIT . . . OKAY!
TEACHING YOUR DOG TO WAIT BEFORE EXITING DOORS

A useful command to teach your dog is to wait at doorways until told it is all right to go through them. This will stand you in good stead if someone accidentally leaves a door to the outdoors open. It will make your dog think twice about bolting through any door, either house door or car door.

Have a thin, light leash about ten feet long on your dog. You can make one with a piece of clothesline rope and a snap, available at hardware stores. Attach the end of the leash to something inside the house that the dog cannot move, such as a doorknob. Be sure that the dog has enough leash length so that he could go out the open door. In case he does, the leash will prevent his running off.

Place your dog, on this leash, inside the house near a door to the outside. With the flat palm of your hand, tap his nose against his nostrils. Say, clearly, three or four times, "Wait!" Then open the door. If your dog makes a leap to go through it, place him again indoors a couple of feet from the door, tap his nose with the flat of your hand against his nostrils, a bit harder than the first time, repeat "Wait!" and open the door. If he again bolts for the door, repeat the exercise, but instead of your hand, use the jumping bat. Be very careful not to get near his eyes with it. Just tap his nose once, then slap the bat with real force on the floor (so the dog will realize that you could have used great force on him, if you had wanted to).

When you can open the door without the dog trying to go through it, say "Okay!" and lead him through the door to the outside. Then turn around and come right back inside. Repeat over and over.

Use this exercise each time the dog is indoors and you are opening a door to the outdoors.

Teach your dog to wait inside the car when you open the door until you give the "Okay" command.

WORMS

Dogs are susceptible to worms of different kinds in all parts of the United States, especially where mosquitoes are present. Fortunately there is treatment or preventive medicine for every kind of worm common to dogs; it is important to take the initiative and either prevent or eliminate the problem.

The most common types of worms that dogs get are hookworms, roundworms, whipworms, tapeworms, and heartworms.

HOOKWORMS

Puppies in particular often have hookworms, which can be passed from the mother to the puppy before birth. A grown dog also can pick up hookworms from unclean areas in which he walks, such as a yard or pen where feces are not picked up frequently. A dog can pick up the larvae on his paws, lick his paws, and get hookworms. If your dog appears to be in poor condition, with a dull coat, lack of energy, and poor muscle condition, you should suspect hookworms or one of the other varieties of worms, and have your vet check him for worms. Vets can identify hookworms from a stool sample that you bring in (in a plastic bag or jar) or from a smear that he takes direct from the dog.

ROUNDWORMS

Because roundworms can infect both other dogs and human beings, especially children who play on or near the ground, it is especially important to eliminate them from your dog. Like hookworms, roundworms often infest puppies, but older dogs may have them and become virtually immune to them, harboring them for years without outward signs. Keeping your dog's environment clean and sanitary is the best line of defense against roundworms. A vet can check your dog's stool sample and prescribe medicine to eliminate the problem.

WHIPWORMS

Also found where dogs live in unsanitary conditions, whipworms can cause diarrhea or a general loss of condition. Dogs pick up whipworms by licking their paws after walking in contaminated areas. A vet will check your dog's stool to determine if whipworms are present and prescribe medicine to eliminate the problem.

A home remedy for hookworms, roundworms, and whipworms is to feed your dog the dark green outer cabbage leaves. You may have to chop them up and mix them with meat if your dog is not used to eating raw vegetables as a snack. The treatment should be repeated daily for a week or two.

TAPEWORMS

If you notice little white worms around your dog's anal area or on his bedding that look something like grains of rice, he probably has tapeworms. A vet will make diagnosis from a stool sample and prescribe medicine for the condition.

Also try feeding dark green cabbage as above.

HEARTWORMS

One of the most serious types of worm infestation to which dogs are susceptible, heartworms are easily prevented by a once-a-month pill (easily fed by wrapping it in cream cheese). A daily pill can be used, but many veterinarians prefer the monthly pill as it is easier to administer and safer for the dog. Some types also protect the dog against hookworms at the same time.

Heartworms are caused by the bite of an infected mosquito. The disease is a threat to dogs nationwide. A preventive medicine is easy to administer and will prevent the disease altogether. A veterinarian will check your dog for presence of the disease (by taking a blood sample) and prescribe pills to prevent it.

Caution: Never give heartworm preventive medicine unless a vet has checked your dog with a blood test first. The pills can kill a dog who is already harboring heartworms, as full-grown worms already in the heart, if killed by medicine, clog the heart's arteries and cause heart failure or stroke.

Signs that a dog has an advanced case of heartworms include a chronic cough, weight loss (ribs show, and a saggy belly is sometimes present, but the dog lacks muscle and flesh on his back and sides), and fatigue. Note that these signs do not generally show up until the disease is well advanced. If any of these signs is present, you should see a vet without delay.

Heartworms are introduced into a dog by a mosquito carrying blood from an infected dog. Immature heartworms circulate in the newly infected dog's bloodstream, migrate through the dog's tissues, and, over a period of several months, reach the dog's heart. Here the worms can grow longer than a foot, causing great damage to heart and lungs.

Fortunately, even an advanced case of heartworm is treatable, although the treatment is expensive and takes about six weeks.

Treatment for heartworm requires that the dog be kept at home absolutely quiet (in a crate, and hand-walked just enough to relieve himself) for the three weeks following treatment with arsenic, which a veterinarian will administer. This initial treatment usually requires the dog to remain in the veterinary hospital for three days as the arsenic solution is dripped slowly into the dog's system via intravenous solution.

The second treatment occurs immediately after the first, and consists of an injection or pills given once only. It does not require a hospital stay. However, the dog must again be kept immobile for another three weeks. The reason for the immobilization, in both cases, is to prevent the killed heartworms (in two different stages of development) from moving through the dog's heart and blocking the flow of blood.

Dogs can and do fully recover from heartworm. But it is far preferable—essential, really—to prevent the disease by giving preventive heartworm medicine. A brand called Heartgard, given monthly, has worked flawlessly for many dogs I have owned or found homes for over the years. Your vet can tell you about new developments in treatment, as products are being continually improved.

Keep careful records of the date you give the medicine (and the name of the dog you give it to each time, if you have more than one dog), and follow the vet's instructions exactly. You will need to give the preventive medicine during all months in which mosquitoes live and one month more after a frost. The medicine works backward—that is, it kills any larvae that have gained access to the dog over the past month.

KATE DELANO CONDAX

Kate Delano Condax has trained dogs—and their human companions to work with them—for more than thirty years.

As an obedience trainer who emphasizes solving specific problems of behavior and general care, she has made life happier and healthier at both ends of the leash for thousands of dogs and their human friends.

For many years she has rescued, rehabilitated, trained, and found loving homes for abused and abandoned dogs. The seven dogs in the illustrations of this book were all rescued from city streets, municipal dumps, and dog pounds.

Kate Delano Condax is author also of *Horse Sense: Cause and Correction of Horse and Rider Problems* (first published in 1979, and republished 1992 by Simon & Schuster) and of an upcoming book for young riders to be published in 1995.

INDEX